Dietmar Prudix

Project Management by numbers

Simple-clear-short-fast

Impressum:

Bibliografische Information der Deutschen Nationalbibliothek:
Die Deutsche Nationalbibliothek verzeichnet diese Publikation in
der Deutschen Nationalbibliografie; detaillierte bibliografische
Daten sind im Internet über www.dnd.de abrufbar.

© 2016 Dietmar Prudix

Herstellung und Verlag:
BoD – Books on Demand, Norderstedt
ISBN 978-3-7431-1390-9

From the same author:

Die eierlegende Wollmilchsau
Die Tage nach dem Bombenwurf
Self Placement
Nehmen Sie die Menschen, so wie sie sind...
The NASA Rules
Co-Author, Kompetenzbasiertes Projektmanagement (PM3): Handbuch für die Projektarbeit
Projektweisheiten

Table of Contents

Forward 7
42 Personal projekt strategies from Napoleon 9
64 Reasons that is project fail 14
5 Definitions of Project Failure 27
22 Types of Project Risk 30
12 Examples Of The Pareto Principle 36
130 Project Management Objectives 44
100 NASA Rules 59
39 Types of Project Risk 76
5 Types of Risk Treatment 85
19 Types of Project Constraint 87
101 Project Management Basics 91
16 Types of Project Stakeholder 109
19 Agile Principles 113
26 Scrum Basics 116
15 Immutable Laws of Project Management 123
10 Project Management Best Practices 126
63 Experts Share Their #1 Tip 131
8 Reasons, Benefits and Overviews 151
9 Lessons Learned from the Apollo 11 Moon Landing 176
7 Top Challenges by Peter Taylor 185
5 Lessons to Learn from Superheroes 191

Forward

Attached you´ll find different perspectives of project management with different insights: The best way to get an access to projects including success factors.

For example Jerry Madden, retired associate director of the flight projects directorate within the NASA`s Goddard Space Flight Center is known as the first project manager in the NASA organization. Over years he collected these gems of wisdom.

Although it`s not part of Jerry`s written lessons learned, he consistently told his people the following: "Show up early for all meetings; they may be serving doughnuts." Finally, Les Meredith (former director of Space Sciences and Acting Center Director) had this remark to make about Jerry Madden`s project managers lessons learned: "God only gave us ten commandments. Jerry has listed over a hundred instructions to a project manager. It is evident a lot more is expected from a project manager"

So the idea was born: Project management by numbers.

Project management is people business. A lot of learnings are linked to well-known people, like Napoleon or some super heroes.

Enjoy

Dietmar Prudix

42 Personal projekt strategies from Napoleon

Planning

1. I start out by believing the worst.

2. The reason most people fail instead of succeed is they trade what they want most for what they want at the moment.

3. There is only one step from the sublime to the ridiculous.

Office Politics

4. Never interrupt your enemy when he is making a mistake.

5. In politics, stupidity is not a handicap.

6. The herd seek out the great, not for their sake but for their influence; and the great welcome them out of vanity or need.

7. When you have an enemy in your power, deprive him of the means of ever injuring you.

8. If they want peace, nations should avoid the pinpricks that precede cannon shots.

9. We frustrate many designs against us by pretending not to see them.

Motivating Teams

10. Give me enough medals and I'll win you any war.

11. A cowardly act! What do I care about that? You may be sure that I should never fear to commit one if it were to my advantage.

12. Courage isn't having the strength to go on - it is going on when you don't have strength.

13. Impossible is a word to be found only in the dictionary of fools.

14. Victory belongs to the most persevering.

Training and Professional Development

15. Show me a family of readers, and I will show you the people who move the world.

Leadership

16. Imagination rules the world.

17. A leader is a dealer in hope.

18. He who fears being conquered is sure of defeat.

19. Ten people who speak make more noise than ten thousand who are silent.

20. Ability is of little account without opportunity.

21. Circumstances-what are circumstances? I make circumstances.

22. Glory is fleeting, but obscurity is forever.

23. In our time no one has the conception of what is great. It is up to me to show them.

24. A true man hates no one.

25. One is more certain to influence men, to produce more effect on them, by absurdities than by sensible ideas.

26. Lead the ideas of your time and they will accompany and support you; fall behind them and they drag you along with them; oppose them and they will overwhelm you.

Work Life Balance

27. Let him sleep … for when he wakes, he will move mountains.

Product Launch

28. The greatest danger occurs at the moment of victory.

Managing Teams

> 29. Never ascribe to malice that which can adequately be explained by incompetence.

> 30. If you want a thing done well, do it yourself.

Managing Stakeholder Expectations

> 31. The best way to keep one's word is not to give it.

Project Communications

> 32. Four hostile newspapers are more to be feared than a thousand bayonets.

Managing Issues

> 33. The battlefield is a scene of constant chaos. The winner will be the one who controls that chaos, both his own and the enemies.

> 34. I may have lost a battle, but not the war.

> 35. In politics nothing is immutable. Events carry within them an invincible power. The unwise destroy themselves in resistance. The skillful accept events, take strong hold of them and direct them.

Decision Making

36. Nothing is more difficult, and therefore more precious, than to be able to decide.
37. Take time to deliberate, but when the time for action comes, stop thinking and go in.

Project Management

38. All great events hang by a hair. The man of ability takes advantage of everything and neglects nothing that can give him a chance of success; whilst the less able man sometimes loses everything by neglecting a single one of those chances.

39. If you wish to be a success in the world, promise everything, deliver nothing.

Risk Management

40. If the art of war were nothing but the art of avoiding risks, glory would become the prey of mediocre minds.... I have made all the calculations; fate will do the rest.

41. Audacity succeeds as often as it fails.

Compliance

42. There are so many laws that no one is safe from hanging.

64 Reasons that is project fail

Testing fails to uncover serious defects that are later detected by users (shaking confidence in the product).

IT projects commonly fail. Studies peg the average project failure rate somewhere between 50%-80%.

In recent years, many organizations have mandated lessons learned sessions for every project. This has led to a better understanding of why projects fail.

Failure often has more than one root cause. In other words, many projects are ripe with problems. The following list (with examples) represents the most common reasons projects fail.

Business Case

1. Failure to evaluate alternatives

The business case fails to consider alternative approaches to the project. This exposes the project to challenges later (i.e. why didn't we consider _____ approach?).

2. Poor financial forecasts

Financial forecasts in the business case are inaccurate.

3. Optimism bias renders business case unrealistic

The business case makes rosy assumptions that don't reflect business realities.

4. Cooked numbers in forecast

Lack of objective financial analysis. The developer of the business case makes the numbers "work".

5. Metric based approvals

Reviewers approve a business case based on a handful of forecast metrics without examining constraints and risks.

6. Missed future costs

The business case promises to reduce existing costs but fails to anticipate new costs the project will introduce. For example, a system project may free-up administrative resources but increase the need for system administrators (who are generally more expensive).

7. No business case

The project proceeds without a formal analysis of its merit.

8. Budgeting errors

A low quality project budget that leads to financial chaos.

9. Poor risk analysis

Failure to identify, analyse and communicate risks.

10. Failure to identify all stakeholders

The project manager fails to involve IT operations. When

it comes time to launch, the head of operations rejects the project.

11. Optimistic resource assumptions

The project plan assumes key resources are 100% committed to the project when they have other commitments.

12. Optimistic estimates

Estimates that are overly optimistic or fail to consider true project scope.

13. Coerced estimates

The project manager directs the team to provide low estimates.

Can you estimate this? I don`t except it that it will take you any longer than few days.

14. Naive estimates

Those who provide estimates don't have the requisite experience (e. g. the project manager provides estimates for the testing phase).

15. Rough estimates

Ballpark estimates are assumed to be rock solid (no formal estimates are produced).

16. Failure to properly estimate tasks not considered critical

Tasks that aren't on the critical path such as data migration are severely underestimated.

17. Poor task scheduling

The work breakdown structure is missing dependencies.

18. Big bang releases

It's well accepted that releasing a project in incremental phases tends to reduce risk and cost. Nevertheless, projects tend to be planned with major releases.

19. No Methodology

The project is executed according to an ad-hoc process that's likely to fail.

Requirements

20. Inadequate requirements

Unclear requirements that leave too much room for interpretation. In many cases, the project manager or developers end up filling in the blanks.

21. Gap between requirements and expectations

Business users begin to dream that the system will do things that aren't captured by the requirements.

22. Requirements aren't compliant

Requirements are not in compliance with laws, regulations, standards, best practices or requisite audits.

23. Silo requirements

Requirements fail to look at the project at the enterprise level. For example, they fail to consider integration with key business processes.

24. Naive requirements

Lack of due diligence in developing and validating requirements (e. g. subject matter experts aren't consulted).

25. Solution in search of a problem

The requirements don't solve business problems.

26. Requirements don't match the business case

The requirements drift from the original goal of the project.

27. Requirements dictate architecture

Requirements specify the solution. For example, specifying that a particular COTS product must be used without proper due diligence.

28. Inaccurate requirement priorities

Nice-to-have requirements are classified as high priority.

Project Execution

29. Project plan becomes outdated

The project plan isn't kept up to date during the execution phase. It quickly becomes obsolete and the project essentially runs without a plan.

30. Tasks aren't tracked

Schedule slippage isn't addressed until deadlines have passed. The project becomes hopelessly behind schedule and over budget.

31. Issues aren't managed

The project manager fails to aggressively escalate and resolve issues.

32. Scope management failure

Severe scope creep throws the project into disarray.

33. Risk realization

A risk identified in the planning phase is realized. For example, a project plan may identify a heavy dependency on a critical resource. If that resource resigns or becomes ill, the risk is realized and the project may fail.

34. Financial controls failure

The project manager fails to control the project budget.

35. Low performance

The performance of a key team member fails to meet expectations.

36. Communication failure

Project goals, objectives, progress; productivity, quality, risk and constraint information isn't transparent to key stakeholders. Expectations become out of line with project reality.

37. Low customer satisfaction

The customers (e. g. project sponsors or users) aren't

happy with the project. For example, executives get the perception that the project is out of control.

Business

38. Business strategy change

New business priorities lead to project cancellation.

39. Business environment

A recession or industry event takes place that triggers project cancellation.

40. Organizational changes

Organizational changes disrupt project execution.

41. Business disruption

Project launch often requires time from key business talent (e. g. learning a new system or launching new business processes). For this reason, there is sometimes resistance to launch.

42. Low user adoption

Users refuse to adopt a new technology or process.

43. Excessive quality sacrifices

Business demands a fast, cheap project. They sign off on risks that the project will have quality issues. The result is a low quality product that's unusable.

44. Negative business results

A project that's delivered to specifications but the business results don't meet expectations. For example, a new product that decreases sales instead of improving sales.

45. Force Majeure

An act of war or nature.

Political

46. Loss of sponsorship

The sponsor changes their mind about the project.

47. Loss of executive support

Powers larger than the sponsor step in to stop the project (sponsor lacks support).

48. Project Infighting

Interpersonal conflict between team members.

49. Passive aggressive tactics

A stakeholder secretly sabotages the project.

50. Vendor management failure

Your relationship with a key vendor turns bad and project issues quickly pile up.

51. Vendor infighting

The relationship between vendors turns bitter and issues mount.

Technical

52. Naive technology selection

Business chooses technologies without understanding the full implications of their decisions.

53. Inadequate technology evaluation

Technologies are chosen without a diligent evaluation.

54. Poor architectural design

The solution architecture is flawed leading to insurmountable project issues.

55. IT governance

IT governance blocks the project. For example, the project duplicates capabilities that already exist.

56. Loss of key technical resources

Losing a key resource who has no backup.

57. Unforeseen technology dependencies

A technology dependency is identified in the execution phase that delays the project.

58. Gold plating

Developers add features to the product that aren't in the

requirements. The added complexity escalates project costs or prompts users to reject the product.

59. Security vulnerabilities

Security vulnerabilities in a chosen technology trigger unforeseen risks, costs and delays.

60. Capacity planning failure

The product fails performance testing and requires hardware or software reworks beyond the project's budget.

61. Tool breakdown

Tools (e. g. development tools) are buggy or ineffective leading to delays.

62. Data quality

The data migration team discovers that data quality is low. The solution is unusable without major data quality initiatives.

63. No methodology

Development follows *an adhoc process that's prone to failure.*

64. Inadequate testing

Testing fails to uncover serious defects that are later detected by users (shaking confidence in the product).

5 Definitions of Project Failure

Most IT professionals will agree that project failure is common. Exactly how common largely depends on the definition of project failure.

Different studies peg the average IT project failure rate between 50%-80%. However, they tend to use differing criteria to define failure.

There are at least 5 common definitions of project failure:

1. Judgment Call

The stakeholders (or some subset of stakeholders) decide if a project is a success or failure. For example, a project board may make this decision as part of project closure activities.

In other words, a project is a failure if its stakeholders consider it a failure. This is the most commonly accepted definition of project failure.

2. Delivery to Plan

Any project that fails to meet time, budget and quality targets is considered a failure.

This is a relatively strict definition that may lead project managers to pad schedules and budgets with excessive contingency.

3. On-time Delivery

Any project that is late is considered a failure.

Organizations in highly competitive, time-to-market driven industries are sometimes tolerant of cost overruns as long as a project meets its target launch date.

4. Financial Results Match Projections

Any project that fails to meet the financial forecasts set out in its business plan is considered a failure.

In many ways, this is the most effective definition. It's hard to mark a successful investment as a failure.

5. Minimum Return

The project fails to meet a minimum return criteria (e.g. a minimum ROI target).

This approach marks a project as successful if it pays back (even if it comes short of the financial forecasts in the business case).

22 Types of Project Risk

When you're young, risk seems like an interesting topic. It sounds like something you might encounter on a snowboard or in a race car.

By the time you've grown up and become a professional project manager, it's equally fascinating.

Project risk management is a project management activity that involves identifying, assessing, measuring, documenting, communicating, avoiding, mitigating, transferring, accepting, controlling and managing risk.

The process of identifying risks is intuitive for experienced project managers. The following types of risks (risk categories) should be enough to stimulate your creativity.

1. Executive Support
Wavering, inconsistent or weak executive commitment is often a project's biggest risk. This can be difficult (but not impossible) to document. Ask for specific commitments. Where you are denied you can document it as a risk.

2. Scope
The quality of your estimates, dependencies and scope management. If an estimate is just a guess, that's a risk. Be sensitive to the comfort level of estimates. If your team is unsure about a particular estimate, you can document this as a risk.

3. Change Management
A continuous flow of complex change requests can escalate the complexity of your project and throw it off course. Change requests may lead to a perception that a project has failed because they continually add budget and time to the project.

If requirements are missing items that are expected to come later, that's a risk.

4. Stakeholders
Stakeholders with a negative attitude towards a project may intentionally throw up roadblocks every step of the way. If you anticipate conflict or a lack of cooperation between stakeholders, document it as a risk.

5. Resources & Team
Resource issues such as turnover and learning curves are common project risks.

There's always a risk that your key experts will leave. If your team are inexperienced or need to acquire new skills, that's another risk.

6. Design
The feasibility and flexibility of architecture and design are key to your project's success.

Low quality design is a risk. You might want to highlight the design of complex or experimental components as separate risks.

7. Technical
The risk that components of your technology stack will be low quality. There are dozens of quality factors for technical components (e.g. stability, availability, scalability, usability, security, extensibility).

It's a good idea to identify specific risks in components. For example, the risk that a component will have a security flaw.

8. Integration
Whatever you're delivering needs to integrate with the processes, systems, organizations, culture and knowledge of the environment. Integration risks are common.

If you need to integrate your project into a business process there's a risk that the process will be disrupted. This may represent a significant business impact. In 1999, a ERP implementation at Hershey's disrupted manufacturing and distribution operations. The company was unable to process $100 million in orders. Quarterly profits dropped 19 percent.

9. Communication
Invalid stakeholder expectations is a fundamental project risk. If the stakeholders think you're building an orange but you're building an apple — your project will fail.

If stakeholders become disengaged (e.g. ignore project communications), that's a risk.

10. Requirements
Garbage in, garbage out. If requirements aren't feasible or are detached from business realities, your project may fail.

Look at the feasibility, quality and completeness of requirements to identify risks. Look at whether requirements are possible to integrate with organizations, processes and systems.

11. Decision Quality
Slow, low quality or ambiguous decisions are common risks.

12. Feasibility
Risk identification is a critical time to consider the feasibility of the project. Ask the key members of your team to do their own sanity checks.

List any doubts about feasibility as risks.

13. Procurement
The procurement process is ripe with risks. For example, there's a risk that you won't find an acceptable proposal to an RFP.

There's also a risk that your vendors won't deliver to the terms of their contracts.

14. Quality
Quality and risk management are intertwined. You'll expect to have defects in your project. However, there's a risk that quality won't meet basic levels. Significant rework may trigger project failure.

Identify quality related risks for process inputs and outputs. Identify quality risks for infrastructure, work packages, components and products.

15. Authority
Project teams often lack authority to complete project work. In many cases, teams are expected to influence to achieve project objectives. This reflects business realities. For example, your project may cross organizational boundaries. It's rare that a project team doesn't depend upon influence.

It's a useful exercise to think of risks in terms of a lack of authority. If you need to influence to secure infrastructure. cooperation or inputs — there's always a chance the answer will be no.

16. Approvals & Red Tape
If you anticipate that red tape (e.g. financial approvals) will slow down your project — add this as a risk.

17. Organizational
Organizational change (e.g. restructuring, mergers, acquisitions) will throw your project off track.

Think about the minimum stability that your products require to launch. List potential organizational changes as risks.

18. External
External forces such as laws, regulations and markets. If your project touches compliance-sensitive processes regulatory change is a risk.

19. Project Management
If your organization asks you to streamline your project management methodology (drop processes and documentation) you can document this as a risk.

20. Secondary Risks
Secondary risks are often overlooked aspect of risk.

Secondary risks are the result of risk mitigation and transfers. Let's say you transfer a risk to a vendor with a fixed price contract. The contract itself represents a counterparty risk. You've replaced a series of project execution risks with a series of procurement risks.

21. User Acceptance
There's always a chance that users will reject your product. You can build a product that matches requirements (on time and to budget). However, if users reject the product the project will be considered a failure.

22. Commercial
If you're building a commercial product for market (new product development), there's always a chance the product will be a commercial failure. This should be documented as a project risk.

12 Examples Of The Pareto Principle

In 1906, Italian economist Vilfredo Pareto noted that 80% of Italy's land was owned by 20% of the people.

He became somewhat obsessed with this ratio, seeing it in everything. For example, he observed that 80% of the peas in his garden came from 20% of his pea plants.

The 80:20 ratio of cause-to-effect became known as the Pareto Principle.

Definition: Pareto Principle

Pareto principle is a prediction that 80% of effects come from 20% of causes.

The pareto principle has become a popular business maxim. It has been used to describe everything from economics to projects.

Common business examples of the pareto principle include:

Projects

> **80% of value is achieved with the first 20% of effort**
>
> Project teams commonly report that a task is almost completed after a short time. A long time may pass after that before they report any further progress.

80% of project politics come from 20% of your stakeholders

Political struggles often originate with a few of your stakeholders.

Program Management

80% of problems originate with 20% of projects

Some projects are far more problematic than others.

Management

80% of work is completed by 20% of your team

The observation that there is often a wide performance gap between your top performers and the rest of your team.

Technology

80% of software problems are caused by 20% of bugs

The observation that most problems are caused by a handful of serious bugs.

80% of customers only use 20% of software features

Most users don't use power features. In many cases, they find power features to be annoying (e.g. complex interfaces).

Sales & Marketing

80% of sales come from 20% of your clients

Many businesses are dependent on their largest accounts.

80% of sales come from 20% of your products

Product diversification may have limited impact on your business.

80% of sales come from 20% of your salespeople

Killer salespeople aren't easy to find.

80% of your complaints come from 20% of your customers

This is a commonly cited customer service rule of thumb.

Wealth Management

80% of wealth is owned by 20% of people

Pareto's 1906 observation that 80% of Italy's wealth (land) was controlled by 20% of people has held up extremely well. Today, 20% of the world's population controls 82.7% of wealth.

General

80% of success is showing up – Woody Allen

The idea that much of success is jumping through the hoops. It has a grain of truth to it. If you consider that "showing up" is 20% of effort — it's an example of the pareto principle.

81 Step Project Management Checklist

The project management checklist below covers the most common project management tasks.

Tasks should be added and subtracted to match the complexity of your project and your project management methodology.

Business Case (document)

1. Business Context
2. Project Overview
3. Project Alternatives
4. Target Business Outcomes
5. Value Proposition (e.g. ROI, net present value, payback period)
6. Assumptions
7. Constraints
8. Risks
9. Deliverables
10. Requested Budget and Financial Schedule

Business Case Review (process)

11. Identify Approvers
12. Communicate Business Case
13. Business Case Review Meeting
14. Business Case Approval
15. Financial Approvals

Feasibility Study (process)

16. Conduct a Feasibility Study

Project Charter (document)

17. Project Objectives
18. Project Benefits
19. Solution Constraints
20. List of Stakeholders
21. Project Organizational Chart
22. Project Scope
23. Out of Scope Items
24. Phase Definitions and Initial Schedule
25. Resource Requirements
26. Initial Communication Plan
27. High Level Risk Management Plan
28. Spending Authority and Initial Budget

Project Charter Review (process)

29. Identify Approvers
30. Communicate Project Charter
31. Project Kickoff Meeting
32. Project Charter Approval

Initiation Phase Review (process)

33. Perform Initiation Phase Review

Project Planning (process)

34. Develop a Resource Plan
35. Obtain Resource Approvals
36. Set Up Project Office
37. Develop Project Management Plan

Project Management Plan (Document)

38. Scope Management Plan
39. Communication Plan
40. Project Budget
41. Risk Management Plan
42. Quality Management Plan
43. Procurement Plan
44. Resource Management Plan
45. Project Change Management Plan
46. Financial Management Plan
47. User Acceptance Plan
48. Work Breakdown Structure
49. Project Schedule (including milestones)

Planning Phase Review (process)

50. Perform Planning Phase Review

Procurement (process)

51. Develop RFI
52. Communicate RFI
53. Review Vendor Responses to RFI
54. Develop RFP
55. Communicate RFP
56. Review Vendor Responses to RFP
57. Select Vendors
58. Negotiate Vendor Contracts

Execution Process (repeated process)

59. Build Deliverables
60. Manage Risk and Issues
61. Control Budget
62. Manage Project Cash Flow
63. Update Project Plan
64. Manage Communication
65. Manage Risks
66. Manage Project Team
67. Manage Project Vendors
68. Manage Quality
69. Manage Change Management
70. Manage User Acceptance

Execution Phase Review (process)

71. Perform Execution Phase Review

Project Closure (process)

72. Evaluate Project Performance
73. Evaluate Individual Performance
74. Perform Lessons Learned
75. Perform Post Implementation Review
76. Identify Outstanding Risks and Issues
77. Handover Project Documentation To Customer
78. Release Project Resources
79. Finalize Vendor Contracts
80. Develop Project Closure Report
81. Communicate Project Closure

130 Project Management Objectives

As a project manager, your primary objective is to achieve project goals. That sounds simple enough at first glance.

However, when projects fail (as they often do) it's important to protect yourself with well designed objectives. Detail your performance objectives in a way that allows your performance to be recognized even when projects fail.

The following examples of project management objectives may help you develop your performance MBO or balance scorecard.

Make your objectives SMART (specific, measurable, achievable, relevant and time-sensitive) within the context of your projects and responsibilities.

1. Primary Objectives

2. Deliver project objectives within time, resource and budget constraints.

3. Align project execution with the strategy, mission, culture and ethics of the organization.

4. Identify and clear project issues.

5. Identify innovative solutions and approaches.

6. Lead teams to motive and energize talent.

7. Sustain a sense of urgency around project critical paths and issues.

8. Persevere to overcome project setbacks.

9. Generate awareness of projects to gather support.

10. Implement strategies to achieve project objectives.

11. Deliver to commitments.

Manage individual time and stress pressures.

12. Integration Management

13. Develop a baseline project plan.

14. Monitor and control project to plan.

15. Manage change to prevent scope creep.

16. Incorporate accepted changes into project plan.

17. Redefine project plan to reflect changes to time, scope, quality, risk and cost priorities.

18. Monitor project execution to plan.

Shutdown projects that are headed for certain failure (recommend re-baselining the project).

19. Scope Management

20. Develop a business case.

21. Investigate project alternatives.

22. Determine project approaches.

23. Develop an opportunity analysis.

24. Define client needs.

25. Identify project objectives and benefits.

26. Determine project specifications.

27. Identify project scope.

28. Subdivide a large project scope into into manageable project phases or subprojects.

29. Develop work breakdown structures and define tasks, components and dependencies.

30. Define project roles and responsibilities.

31. Define project tasks and deliverables.

32. Develop time, cost and resource estimates.

33. Ensure that project activities are aligned with client objectives.

34. Develop and communicate a scope statement that defines project work and limits.

35. Develop a project charter.

36. Manage project charter approvals.

37. Identify and control changes that impact scope such as requirements changes.

38. Monitor project progress to plan.

39. Manage scope problems.

40. Communicate and escalate scope issues.

Time Management

41. Prepare a baseline project schedule.

42. Estimate effort and time.

43. Identify dependencies.

44. Identify resource requirements.

45. Schedule project work, gates and milestones.

46. Identify and manage critical paths.

47. Calculate probabilities of meeting project dates.

48. Control project schedule.

49. Report schedule performance.

50. Determine impact of delayed or early tasks.

51. Control scope changes and impact to schedule.

52. Manage change and revise schedule as required.

53. Manage resource utilization.

Cost Management

54. Prepare project budget.

55. Manage budget approvals.

56. Control project budget.

57. Manage project cash flow.

58. Assess impact of scope changes to budget.

59. Control changes to project budget.

60. Develop cash flow forecasts.

61. Calculate probabilities of cost variances.

62. Account for costs by task, time period and cost account.

63. Report cost performance using methods such as earned value.

64. Communicate costs and manage stakeholder cost

Quality Management

65. Identify quality control standards (e.g. ISO 9001).

66. Ensure project complies with quality control standards.

67. Develop a quality management plan.

68. Manage quality assurance.

69. Measure and report quality of project deliverables.

Human Resource Management

70. Assemble teams according to project needs.

71. Establish visions and principles for teams.

72. Establish a team culture that allows teams to achieve objectives.

73. Identify training needs for projects.

74. Plan and schedule training and development.

75. Set achievable, measurable, realistic objectives for team members.

76. Negotiation goals and expectations with team members.

77. Facilitate cooperation, openness and creativity.

78. Motivate teams and inspire a sense of teamwork, ownership and urgency.

79. Involve team members in decision making to achieve acceptance of decisions and approaches.

80. Develop leaders and support the career growth of team members.

81. Provide timely recognition of team and individual achievements.

82. Provide timely constructive performance feedback to improve performance issues early.

83. Mentor team members and new project managers.

Communications Management

84. Gain commitment to decisions and approaches by promoting open dialog between stakeholders.

85. Present complex issues clearly.

86. Model decisions for stakeholders.

87. Adapt your communication style to each situation.

88. Handle confidential and private information appropriately.

89. Proactively communicate potential issues.

90. Run efficient meetings using time management best practices.

91. Develop meaningful project measurements and KPIs and report them regularly.

92. Create meaningful project dashboards that provide project transparency to all stakeholders.

Risk Management

93. Identify risks with stakeholders.

94. Compare identified risks with lists of well known project risks to ensure completeness.

95. Evaluate risk probabilities and impacts.

96. Evaluate risk interactions and assess possible risk outcomes.

97. Prioritize risks based on probability, impact and stakeholder priorities.

98. Identify risk controls.

99. Identify contingency plans.

100. Develop a risk management plan.

101. Apply risks to cost and time estimates to develop confidence levels.

102. Communicate risks and possible outcomes to stakeholders.

103. Gain acceptance for risk management plan.

104. Monitor and proactively manage risk.

105. Track and report risks according to the risk management plan.

106. Manage risk events.

Procurement Management

107. Develop procurement requirements and plans such as specifications, statements of work, RFIs and RFPs.

108. Liaison with procurement teams and follow organizational best practices and processes.

109. Comply with procurement regulations.

110. Identify short lists of preferred suppliers.

111. Conduct proposal assessments and select proposals.

112. Ensure that proposal selection is objective and fair.

113. Ensure that proposal selection criteria and scoring are well documented.

114. Approve subcontracts.

115. Manage vendors to ensure that they meet the terms of contracts.

116. Control change to contracts.

117. Manage vendor relationships to ensure open communication and positive working relationships.

118. Monitor and report on vendor performance including cost, schedule, scope, quality and risk criteria.

119. Terminate contracts for non-performance.

120. Ensure payments based on milestones such as deliverables and accomplishments as per agreements.

121. Close out contracts and finalize payments.

122. Evaluate, document, communicate and socialize vendor performance.

Stakeholder Management

123. Meet or exceed stakeholder needs.

124. Develop organizational awareness (e.g. an understanding of the organization's structure and politics).

125. Apply an understanding of organizational realities to achieve project goals.
126. Build and maintain a network of alliances to achieve project goals.

127. Influence decision makers to clear project issues and roadblocks.

128. Actively manage stakeholders to resolve issues and conflict.

129. Ensure that stakeholder expectations are in line with project realities.

130. Stand up for the project's objectives to ensure that decisions don't shipwreck the project

100 NASA Rules

The Project Manager

Rule #1: A project manager should visit everyone who is building anything for his project at least once, should know all the managers on his project (both government and contractor), and know the integration team members. People like to know that the project manager is interested in their work and the best proof is for the manager to visit them and see first hand what they are doing.

Rule #2: A project manager must know what motivates the project contractors (i.e., their award system, their fiscal system, their policies, and their company culture).

Rule #3: Management principles still are the same. It is just that the tools have changed. You still find the right people to do the work and get out of the way so they can do it.

Rule #4: Whoever you deal with, deal fairly. Space is not a big playing field. You may be surprised how often you have to work with the same people. Better they respect you than carry a grudge.

Rule #5: Vicious, despicable, or thoroughly disliked persons, gentlemen, and ladies can be project managers. Lost souls, procrastinators, and wishy-washies cannot.

Rule #6: A comfortable project manager is one waiting for his next assignment or one on the verge of failure. Security is not normal to project management.

Rule #7: One problem new managers face is that everyone wants to solve their problems. Old managers were told by senior management—"solve your own darn problems, that is what we hired you to do."

Rule #8: Running fast does not take the place of thinking for yourself. You must take time to smell the roses. For your work, you must take time to understand the consequences of your actions.

Rule #9: The boss may not know how to do the work but he has to know what he wants. The boss had better find out what he expects and wants if he doesn't know. A blind leader tends to go in circles.

Rule #10: Not all successful managers are competent and not all failed managers are incompetent. Luck still plays a part in success or failure but luck favors the competent hard working manager.

Rule #11: Never try to get even for some slight by anyone on the project. It is not good form and it puts you on the same level as the other person and, besides, probably ends up hurting the project getting done.

Rule #12: Don't get too egotistical so that you can't change your position, especially if your personnel tell you that you are wrong. You should cultivate an attitude on the project where your personnel know they can tell you of wrong decisions.

Rule #13: A manager who is his own systems engineer or financial manager is one who will probably try to do open heart surgery on himself.

Rule #14: Most managers succeed on the strength and skill of their staff.

Initial Work

Rule #15: The seeds of problems are laid down early. Initial planning is the most vital part of a project. The review of most failed projects or project problems indicate the disasters were well planned to happen from the start.

Communications

Rule #16: Cooperative efforts require good communications and early warning systems. A project manager should try to keep his partners aware of what is going on and should be the one who tells them first of any rumour or actual changes in plan. The partners should be consulted before things are put in final form, even if they only have a small piece of the action. A project manager who blindsides his partners will be treated in kind and will be considered a person of no integrity.

Rule #17: Talk is not cheap; but the best way to understand a personnel or technical problem is to talk to the right people. Lack of talk at the right levels is deadly.

Rule #18: Most international meetings are held in English. This is a foreign language to most participants such as Americans, Germans, Italians, etc. It is important to have adequate discussions so that there are no misinterpretations of what is said.

Rule #19: You cannot be ignorant of the language of the area you manage or with that of areas with which you interface. Education is a must for the modern manager. There are simple courses available to learn computerese, communicationese and all the rest of the modern "ese's" of the world. You can't manage if you don't understand what is being said or written.

People

Rule #20: You cannot watch everything. What you can watch is the people. They have to know you will not accept a poor job.

Rule #21: We have developed a set of people whose self interest is more paramount than the work or at least it appears so to older managers. It appears to the older managers that the newer ones are more interested in form than in substance. The question is are old managers right or just old? Consider both viewpoints.

Rule #22: A good technician, quality inspector, and straw boss are more important in obtaining a good product than all the paper and reviews.

Rule #23: The source of most problems is people, but darned if they will admit it. Know the people working on your project to know what the real weak spots are.

Rule #24: One must pay close attention to workaholics— if they get going in the wrong direction, they can do a lot of damage in a short time. It is possible to overload them and cause premature burnout but hard to determine if the load is too much, since much of it is self generated. It is important to make sure such people take enough time off and that the workload does not exceed 1 1/4 to 1 1/2 times what is normal.

Rule #25: Always try to negotiate your internal support at the lowest level. What you want is the support of the person doing the work, and the closer you can get to him in negotiations the better.

Rule #26: If you have someone who doesn't look, ask, and analyze; ask them to transfer.

Rule #27: Personal time is very important. You must be careful as a manager that you realize the value of other people's time (i.e., the work you hand out and meetings should be necessary). You must, where possible, shield your staff from unnecessary work (i.e., some requests should be ignored or a refusal sent to the requestor).

Rule #28: People who monitor work and don't help get it done never seem to know exactly what is going on (being involved is the key to excellence).

Rule #29: There is no greater motivation than giving a good person his piece of the puzzle to control, but a pat on the back or an award helps.

Rule #30: It is mainly the incompetent that don't like to show off their work.

Rule #31: There are rare times when only one man can do the job. These are in technical areas that are more art and skill than normal. Cherish these people, but get their work done as soon as possible. Getting the work done by someone else takes two or three times longer and the product is normally below standard.

Rule #32: People have reasons for doing things the way they do them. Most people want to do a good job and, if they don't, the problem is they probably don't know how or exactly what is expected.

Rule #33: If you have a problem that requires additional people to solve, you should approach putting people on like a cook who has under-salted the food.

Reviews and Reports

Rule #34: NASA has established a set of reviewers and a set of reviews. Once firmly established, the system will fight to stay alive, so make the most of it. Try to find a way for the reviews to work for you.

Rule #35: The number of reviews is increasing but the knowledge transfer remains the same; therefore, all your charts and presentation material should be constructed with this fact in mind. This means you should be able to construct a set of slides that only needs to be shuffled from presentation to presentation.

Rule #36: Hide nothing from the reviewers. Their reputation and yours is on the line. Expose all the warts and pimples. Don't offer excuses—just state facts.

Rule #37: External reviews are scheduled at the worst possible time, therefore, keep an up-to-date set of business and technical data so that you can rapidly respond. Not having up-to-date data should be cause for dismissal.

Rule #38: Never undercut your staff in public (i.e., In public meetings, don't reverse decisions on work that you have given them to do). Even if you direct a change, never take the responsibility for implementing away from your staff.

Rule #39: Reviews are for the reviewed an not the reviewer. The review is a failure if the reviewed learn nothing from it.

Rule #40: A working meeting has about six people attending. Meetings larger than this are for information transfer (management science has shown that, in a group greater than twelve, some are wasting their time).

Rule #41: The amount of reviews and reports are proportional to management's understanding (i.e., the less management knows or understands the activities, the more they require reviews and reports). It is necessary in this type of environment to make sure that data is presented so that the average person, slightly familiar with activities, can understand it. Keeping the data simple and clear never insults anyone's intelligence.

Rule #42: Managers who rely only on the paperwork to do the reporting of activities are known failures.

Rule #43: Documentation does not take the place of knowledge. There is a great difference in what is supposed to be, what is thought to have happened, and reality. Documents are normally a static picture in time that get outdated rapidly.

Rule #44: Just because you give monthly reports, don't think that you can abbreviate anything in a yearly report.

If management understood the monthlies, they wouldn't need a yearly.

Rule #45: Abbreviations are getting to be a pain. Each project now has a few thousand. This calls on senior management to know hundreds. Use them sparingly in presentations unless your objective is to confuse.

Rule #46: Remember, it is often easier to do foolish paperwork that to fight the need for it. Fight only if it is a global issue which will save much future work.

Contractors and Contracting

Rule #47: A project manager is not the monitor of the contractor's work but is to be the driver. In award fee situations, the government personnel should be making every effort possible to make sure the contractor gets a high score (i.e., be on schedule and produce good work). Contractors don't fail, NASA does and that is why one must be proactive in support. This is also why a low score damages the government project manager as much as the contractor's manager because it means that he is not getting the job done.

Rule #48: Award fee is a good tool that puts discipline both on the contractor and the government. The score given represents the status of the project as well as the management skills of both parties. The project management measurement system (PMS) should be used to verify the scores. Consistent poor scores require senior management intervention to determine the reason. Consistent good scores which are consistent with PMS reflect a well-run project, but if these scores are not consistent with the PMS, senior management must take action to find out why.

Rule #49: Morale of the contractor's personnel is important to a government manager. Just as you don't want to buy a car built by disgruntled employees, you don't want to buy flight hardware developed by under-motivated people. You should take an active role in motivating all personnel on the project.

Rule #50: Being friendly with a contractor is fine—being a friend of a contractor is dangerous to your objectivity.

Rule #51: Remember, your contractor has a tendency to have a one-on-one interface with your staff. Every member of your staff costs you at least one person on the contract per year.

Rule #52: Contractors tend to size up the government counterparts and staff their part of the project accordingly. If they think yours are clunkers, they will take their poorer people to put on your project.

Rule #53: Contractors respond well to the customer that pays attention to what they are doing but not too well to the customer that continually second-guesses their activity. The basic rule is a customer is always right but the cost will escalate if a customer always has things done his way instead of how the contractor planned on doing it. The ground rule is: never change a contractor's plans unless they are flawed or too costly (i.e., the old saying that better is the enemy of good).

Rule #54: There is only one solution to a weak project manager in industry—get rid of him fast. The main job of a project manager in industry is to keep the customer happy. Make sure the one working with you knows that it is not flattery but on-schedule, on-cost, and a good product that makes you happy.

Engineers and Scientists

Rule #55: Over-engineering is common. Engineers like puzzles and mazes. Try to make them keep their designs simple.

Rule #56: The first sign of trouble comes from the schedule or the cost curve. Engineers are the last to know they are in trouble. Engineers are born optimists.

Rule #57: The project has many resources within itself. There probably are five or ten system engineers considering all the contractors and instrument developers. This is a powerful resource that can be used to attack problems.

Rule #58: Many managers, just because they have the scientists under contract on their project, forget that the scientists are their customers and many times have easier access to top management than the managers do.

Rule #59: Most scientists are rational unless you endanger their chance to do their experiment. They will work with you if they believe you are telling them the truth. This includes reducing their own plans.

Hardware

Rule #60: In the space business, there is no such thing as previously flown hardware. The people who build the next unit probably never saw the previous unit. There are probably minor changes (perhaps even major changes); the operational environment has probably changed; the people who check the unit out in most cases will not understand the unit or the test equipment.

Rule #61: Most equipment works as built, not as the designer planned. This is due to layout of the design, poor understanding on the designer's part, or poor understanding of component specifications.

Computers and Software

Rule #62: Not using modern techniques, like computer systems, is a great mistake, but forgetting that the computer simulates thinking is a still greater mistake.

Rule #63: Software has now taken on all the parameters of hardware (i.e., requirement creep, high percentage of flight mission cost, need for quality control, need for validation procedures, etc.). It has the added feature that it is hard as blazes to determine it is not flawed. Get the basic system working first and then add the bells and whistles. Never throw away a version that works even if you have all the confidence in the world that the newer version works. It is necessary to have contingency plans for software.

Rule #64: Knowledge is often revised by simulations or testing, but computer models have hidden flaws not the least of which is poor input data.

Rule #65: In olden times, engineers had hands-on experience, technicians understood how the electronics worked and what it was supposed to do, and layout technicians knew too—but today only the computer knows for sure and it's not talking.

Senior Management, Program Offices, and Above

Rule #66: Don't assume you know why senior management has done something. If you feel you need to know, ask. You get some amazing answers that will astonish you.

Rule #67: Know your management—some like a good joke, others only like a joke if they tell it.

Rule #68: Remember the boss has the right to make decisions. Even if you think they are wrong, tell the boss what you think but if he still wants it done his way; do it his way and do your best to make sure the outcome is successful.

Rule #69: Never ask management to make a decision that you can make. Assume you have the authority to make decisions unless you know there is a document that states unequivocally that you can't.

Rule #70: You and the Program Manager should work as a team. The Program Manager is your advocate at NASA HQ and must be tied into the decision makers and should aid your efforts to be tied in also.

Rule #71: Know who the decision makers on the program are. It may be someone outside who has the ear of Congress or the Administrator, or the Associate Administrator, or one of the scientists—someone in the chain of command—whoever they are. Try to get a line of communication to them on a formal or informal basis.

Program Planning, Budgeting, and Estimating

Rule #72: Today one must push the state of the art, be within budget, take risks, not fail, and be on time. Strangely, all these are consistent as long as the ground rules such as funding profile and schedule are established up front and maintained.

Rule #73: Most of yesteryear's projects overran because of poor estimates and not because of mistakes. Getting better estimates will not lower costs but will improve NASA's business reputation. Actually, there is a high probability that getting better estimates will increase costs and assure a higher profit to industry unless the fee is reduced to reflect lower risk on the part of industry. A better reputation is necessary in the present environment.

Rule #74: All problems are solvable in time, so make sure you have enough schedule contingency—if you don't, the next project manager that takes your place will.

Rule #75: The old NASA pushed the limits of technology and science; therefore, it did not worry about requirements creep or overruns. The new NASA has to work as if all projects are fixed price; therefore, requirement creep has become a deadly sin.

Rule #76: Know the resources of your center and, if possible, other centers. Other centers, if they have the resources , are normally happy to help. It is always surprising how much good help one can get by just asking.

Rule #77: Other than budget information prior to the President's submittal to Congress, there is probably no secret information on a project—so don't treat anything like it is secret. Everyone does better if they can see the whole picture so don't hide any of it from anyone.

Rule #78: NASA programs compete for budget funds—they do not compete with each other (i.e., you never attack any other program or NASA work with the idea that you should get their funding). Sell what you have on its own merit.

Rule #79: Next year is always the year with adequate funding and schedule. Next year arrives on the 50th year of your career.

The Customer

Rule #80: Remember who the customer is and what his objectives are (i.e., check with him when you go to change anything of significance).

NASA Management Instructions

Rule #81: NASA Management Instructions were written by another NASA employee like you; therefore, challenge them if they don't make sense. It is possible another NASA employee will rewrite them or waive them for you.

Decision Making

Rule #82: Wrong decisions made early can be recovered from. Right decisions made late cannot correct them.

Rule #83: Sometimes the best thing to do is nothing. It is also occasionally the best help you can give. Just listening is all that is needed on many occasions. You may be the boss, but if you constantly have to solve someone's problems, you are working for him.

Rule #84: Never make a decision from a cartoon. Look at the actual hardware or what real information is available such as layouts. Too much time is wasted by people trying to cure a cartoon whose function is to explain the principle.

Professional Ethics and Integrity

Rule #85: Integrity means your subordinates trust you.

Rule #86: In the rush to get things done, it's always important to remember who you work for. Blindsiding the boss will not be to your benefit in the long run.

Project Management and Teamwork

Rule #87: Projects require teamwork to succeed. Remember, most teams have a coach and not a boss, but the coach still has to call some of the plays.

Rule #88: Never assume someone knows something or has done something unless you have asked them; even the obvious is overlooked or ignored on occasion, especially in a high stress activity.

Rule #89: Whoever said beggars can't be choosers doesn't understand project management, although many times it is better to trust to luck than to get poor support.

Rule #90: A puzzle is hard to discern from just one piece; so don't be surprised if team members deprived of information reach the wrong conclusion.

Rule #91: Remember, the President, Congress, OMB, NASA HQ, senior center management, and your customers all have jobs to do. All you have to do is keep them all happy.

Treating and Avoiding Failures

Rule #92: In case of a failure:

- a) Make a timeline of events and include everything that is known.
- b) Put down known facts. Check every theory against them.
- c) Don't beat the data until it confesses (i.e., know when to stop trying to force-fit a scenario).
- d) Do not arrive at a conclusion too fast. Make sure any deviation from normal is explained. Remember the wrong conclusion is prologue to the next failure.
- e) Know when to stop.

Rule #93: Things that fail are lessons learned for the future. Occasionally things go right: these are also lessons learned. Try to duplicate that which works.

Rule #94: Mistakes are all right but failure is not. Failure is just a mistake you can't recover from; therefore, try to create contingency plans and alternate approaches for the items or plans that have high risk.

Rule #95: History is prologue. There has not been a project yet that has not had a parts problem despite all the qualification and testing done on parts. Time and being prepared to react are the only safeguards.

Rule #96: Experience may be fine but testing is better. Knowing something will work never takes the place of proving that it will.

Rule #97: Don't be afraid to fail or you will not succeed, but always work at your skill to recover. Part of that skill is knowing who can help.

Rule #98: One of the advantages of NASA in the early days was the fact that everyone knew that the facts we were absolutely sure of could be wrong.

Rule #99: Redundancy in hardware can be a fiction. We are adept at building things to be identical so that if one fails, the other will also fail. Make sure all hardware is treated in a build as if it were one of a kind and needed for mission success.

Rule #100: Never make excuses; instead, present plans of actions to be taken.

39 Types of Project Risk

Project risks are uncertainties that exposes a project to potential failure to achieve its goals.

Identifying, evaluating and treating risks is an ongoing project management activity that seeks to improve project results by avoiding, reducing or transferring risks. Project risk management also provides stakeholders with visibility and clarifies accountability for accepted risks.

The following are a few types of risk commonly encountered by projects.

1. Scope Creep

Scope creep is uncontrolled change to a project's scope. For example, urgent projects may be attempted on a best effort basis that neglects rigorous management of project change.

2. Budget Risk

The risk of budget control issues such as cost overruns. Budget estimates are based on forward-looking estimates that typically involve some degree of uncertainty.

3. Resistance To Change

Resistance to change is a common occurrence whereby departments and individuals defend the status quo and actively resist projects or organizational changes.

4. Integration Risk

Activities involving integration of technologies, information, processes or organizations tend to be particularly high risk and are often underestimated.

5. Resource Risk

The inability to secure sufficient resources such as skilled workers and budget.

6. Contract Risk

The risk that a counterparty such as a contractor will fail to deliver on their contractual obligations to you.

7. Disputes

The risk of disputes that delay the project that potentially progress to litigation.

8. Sponsor Support

Risks related to the responsibilities of the project sponsor.

9. Technology Risk

Technology risks such as service outages that disrupt the project.

10. Schedule Risk

Schedules usually incorporate a significant degree of uncertainty including forward-looking estimates and assumptions.

11. Project Dependencies

Project dependencies can be evaluated for risk. For example, a task that is a precondition for a large number of activities might be identified as a risk.

12. Project Assumptions

Any potential that project assumptions will be invalidated can be documented as risks.

13. Skills Risk

Risks related to training, skill transfers or resources who are inexperienced at a particular task.

14. Architecture Risk

Architecture risk is the potential failure of new or existing architecture to support project requirements.

15. Stakeholders

Any risks related to stakeholders fulfilling their commitments to the project.

16. Operations Risk

Operations Risk is a failure of an organization's core processes. It is a particularly sensitive area of risk because operational disruptions can result in costs, revenue loss and damage to reputation. Projects that touch core business processes often perform a detailed analysis of operational risks.

17. Benefit Shortfall

In some cases, a project delivers to requirements but is viewed as a failure because it fails to meet the benefits stated in its business case. These risks can be documented as project risks.

18. Exchange Rates

If your budget involves payments or revenue in multiple currencies there is typically an associated exchange rate risk.

19. Health & Safety

Health & safety is a special category of risk that requires alignment with the best practices of your organization and industry. Health and safety is typically granted priority over other project concerns and has compliance implications.

20. Legal Risk

Any risk of future litigation related to your project.

21. Quality Risk

Risks related to the quality of project inputs or outputs.

22. Requirements Quality

If your requirements are low quality or haven't been properly validated these factors can be documented as risks.

23. Project Complexity

Complexity is a function of the size and intricacy of a project relative to the capabilities of your organization. It is a known risk factor that complex projects are generally more likely to fail.

24. Force Majeure

The chance of a major negative event beyond the control of your organization such as a war or earthquake.

25. Supplier Risk

The potential that a supplier will fail to meet their obligations to you such as timely delivery of orders.

26. Regulatory Risk

The possibility of new regulations that impact your project. Particularly relevant if your project is implementing compliance related functions.

27. Procurement Risk

The risk of failure of a procurement process such a request for proposal.

28. Security Risk

The risk of a physical or information security incident.

29. Project Estimates

It is common for project estimates to be a significant source of schedule risk. This relates both to the quality of estimates and to the inherent uncertainty of forward looking estimates.

30. Political Risk

The chance of a political event that disrupts your project.

31. Design Risk

The potential that a design will fail to meet requirements or will be rejected by stakeholders.

32. Infrastructure Risk

Risks associated with the infrastructure needs of the project such as roads required to access a construction site.

33. Program Risk

Program risks that impact your project or vice versa.

34. Reputational Risk

Any major exposures the project has that could potentially impact the reputation of the sponsoring business.

35. Partner Risk

The potential for a partner to fail to meet their obligations to the project.

36. Information Security Risk

Any risk that your project will introduce information security vulnerabilities.

37. Facility Risk

Availability of facilities for the project such as offices or data centers.

38. Market Risk

Market risks such as the price of a commodity. Market conditions are a common cause of benefit shortfall whereby a project fails to achieve its stated business results.

39. Project Planning Risk

The potential for project management itself to fail. This is typically documented as a risk when the project manager is required to take short cuts that deviate from the established best practices of an organization or industry.

5 Types of Risk Treatment

A risk treatment is an action that is taken to manage a risk. Risk management processes all include steps to identify, assesses and then treat risks. In general, there are four types of risk treatment:

1. Avoidance

You can choose not to take on the risk by avoiding the actions that cause the risk. For example, if you feel that swimming is too dangerous you can avoid the risk by not swimming.

2. Reduction

You can take mitigation actions that reduce the risk. For example, wearing a life jacket when you swim.

3. Transfer

You can transfer all or part of the risk to a third party. The two main types of transfer are insurance and outsourcing. For example, a company may choose to transfer a collection of project risks by outsourcing the project.

4. Acceptance

Risk acceptance, also known as risk retention, is choosing to face a risk. In general, it is impossible to profit in business or enjoy an active life without choosing to take on risk. For example, an investor may accept the risk that a company will go bankrupt when they purchase its bonds.

5. Sharing

Risk sharing is the distribution of risk to multiple organizations or individuals. This is done for a variety of reasons including insurance products and self-insurance strategies.

Residual Risk

Risk treatments don't necessarily reduce risks to zero. Remaining risk after treatment is known as residual risk.

Secondary Risk

It's common for your efforts to reduce risk to have risks of their own. These are known as secondary risks. For example, if you outsource a project you will assume a number of secondary risks such as the risk that the outsourcing company will fail to deliver.

19 Types of Project Constraint

A project constraint is a definite and inflexible limitation or restriction on a project. All constraints are tradeoffs. If you constrain budget, the project may be low quality. If you constrain time, you may face risks if the project is rushed. If you constrain risk, the project may be slow and expensive. In some cases, the constraints of a project are impossible. It is easy to see this in an extreme example such the constraints that a building cost $1 and be completed in one day with no risk.

As constraints restrict project options and can result in severe tradeoffs, they demand careful consideration. In most cases, constraints are driven by absolute business necessity. The following is a list of common project constraints.

Business

> Business constraints include anything that the business can't change that affects a project. For example, a business may have commitments to partners, customers or regulators.

Cost

1. A limited budget is an extremely common constraint.
2. An imposed design approach or condition that is beyond the project to change.

Due Diligence

3. Due diligence is the level of care, judgement and investigation that can be reasonably expected of an organization or professional. As due diligence is a legal requirement or professional ethic it generally can't be skipped to expedite a project.

Facilities

4. A limit or restriction on a facility such as a data center.

Human Resources

5. Staffing constraints such as a fixed size team.

6. Infrastructure

7. Use of existing infrastructure that has constraints such as capacity limitations, speed or functionality.

Legal

8. Laws, regulations or agreements that restrict project options.thodology

9. The imposed requirement to use a particular approach such as a project management methodology.

Organizational

10. An organizational constraint such as the need to share resources with functional managers.

Physical

11. A physical constraint such as the size of land or floor space available in a data center.

12. A requirement to adhere to a process such as a budgeting process with cut-off dates.

13. Procurement practices, procedures or processes that must be followed.

14. A quality condition or specification that is a mandatory requirement.

15. Resource constraints such as the power capacity of a data center.

16. The amount of risk that the sponsor is willing to take on.

Scope

17. The minimum scope of a project such as a particular set of requirements.

18. An imposed technology constraint that's beyond the authority of the project to change such as a platform that must be used.

19. A date that must be met.

101 Project Management Basics

Project management is the practice of planning, directing and controlling resources to deliver a project. It is a mature profession and practice that is associated with a number of methodologies, tools and techniques. The following is an overview of project management basics.

Acceptance Criteria

1. A set of conditions for accepting project deliverables. Helps to avoid arbitrary or frivolous rejection of project outputs.

Activity

2. A distinct package of project work.

Assumptions

3. Documented facts, statements or interpretations that are reasonably expected to hold true for the purposes of a project. Agreeing on project assumptions is a fundamental way to align expectations amongst stakeholders.

4. An approved version of requirements and other project documents that serve as a basis for project

work. Requirements not in the baseline are handled as change requests.

Business Analysis

5. The practice of researching business goals, capabilities and processes to develop project artifacts such as requirements.

Business Case

6. A project proposal that is often used as a source document for project artifacts such as a project charter.

Change Control

7. A process whereby changes to baseline requirements and project documents are identified, documented and reviewed. Approved change requests often impact project scope and schedule.

Change Control Board

8. A formally identified group that governs and manages the change control process.

Control System

9. A set of procedures and tools for managing the change control process. Includes a procedure for submitting change requests.

Change Request

10. A formal proposal to change baseline requirements or any other aspect of a project such as an assumption.

Communications Log

11. A running list that details all project communications that have occurred.

Communications Management Plan

12. Describes the process, timing and responsibilities for disseminating project information.

Cone Of Uncertainty

13. A model for project uncertainty whereby projects begin with a great deal of uncertainty that gradually declines as the project progresses.

Configuration Management

14. Procedures and tools for managing change to project artifacts including access control, tracking, versioning, audit trail and monitoring.

Constraint

15. A limit or restriction on a project such as budget, resources or time.

Contingency Plan

16. A plan listing actions the project team can take if risks are triggered.

Contingency Reserve

17. Resources such as time and money built into baseline budgets and plans to handle issues should they occur.

Action

18. Actions that are taken to correct an issue when it occurs.

Cost Baseline

19. An approved version of estimates and contingency reserve that general correspond to an approved version of requirements.

Cost Management Plan

20. A plan that describes how costs will be estimated, budgeted and controlled.

Cost Variance

21. The difference between budgeted and actual costs at a point in time. Often expressed as the ratio of earned value to actual cost.

Crashing

22. Adding resources to a project in an attempt to speed things up.

Critical Path

23. Looking at the minimum time that your project will take to complete by determining your longest path of dependencies between activities.

24. An activity that is on your critical path. That is to say, a member in the longest path of dependencies between activities.

Critical Path Method

25. Analysis of the critical path to determine scheduling options.

Decomposition

26. Dividing projects or activities into smaller parts to make them more manageable. In many cases, large scale projects are more likely to fail than small, quick iterations of smaller projects that achieve the same end results.

Defect

27. A nonconformance to requirements.

28. A verifiable tangible or intangible result of work. In other words, something that is delivered to the customer as part of a project.

Dependency

29. A logical relationship between activities usually described as finish-to-start, finish-to-finish, start-to-start or start-to-finish.

Earned Value

30. A measure of work performed expressed in terms of the budget authorized for that work.

31. The labor required to complete an activity often expressed in days.

32. The estimated cost to complete remaining project work.

Feasibility Study

33. An investigation of a project or requirement to see if it is technically, economically and legally feasible.

Estimates

34. Projections of costs, task completion times and resource needs for a project broken down by activity.
ing
35. An attempt to compress a schedule by doing tasks in parallel that are normally done in sequence.

36. An organization that grouped by specialization such as information technology and accounting. Implies the project manager has limited authority to assign work and resources.

37. A risk that occurs or is about to occur.

38. A document that captures the knowledge gained by a project including an account of what happened and what could have been improved.

39. The duration of a task that doesn't produce a deliverable and isn't on the critical path of a project. Associated with management activities such as budget administration.

Matrix Organization

40. An organizational structure with multiple reporting lines as opposed to a tradition hierarchy. Implies the project manager temporarily shares authority to assign work with functional managers.

Milestone

41. A significant point or event in a project or program.

Most Likely Duration

42. An estimate of the most probable project duration that takes into account risks and constraints.

Organizational Breakdown Structure

43. A hierarchical representation of a project organization that depicts the relationship between project activities and organizational units.

44. The organization that is most directly involved in doing the work of the project.

Phase

45. A distinct stage in a project associated with a number of logically related deliverables.

Phase Gate

46. A review held at the end of a phase to review progress. At each gate an explicit choice is made to continue with the next phase, continue with changes or end the project.

Planned Value

47. The authorized budget that is assigned to schedule work.

Portfolio Management

48. The management of a group of related programs, projects and operations.

Preventive Action

49. An advance action that is taken to prevent an issue or improve project execution.

Management Plan

50. A plan to manage the procurement of project resources, goods and services.

Program

51. A group of related projects and activities that are managed in a coordinated way.

Program Management

52. The direction, coordination and control of a group of related projects and activities.

Project Budget

53. A budget for a work package including contingency reserves.

Project Calendar

54. A calendar of days that are available for project work.

Project Charter

55. A document created by the project sponsor that outlines the scope, objectives, roles and responsibilities of a project. The project charter serves to initiate a project.

Project Management Office

56. A team that standardizes project management practices, processes, tools and techniques for an organization.

Project Management Plan

57. A document that guides the execution and control of a project. Typically includes assumptions, decisions, scope, cost and schedule baselines. In many cases, artifacts such as a communication plan or risk management plan are bundled with the project management plan.

Projectized Organization

58. An organization in which the project manager has full authority to assign work.

Quality Management Plan

59. A plan for directing and controlling project quality.

Requirements

60. A specification of a need or want.

Requirements Management Plan

61. A plan for the analysis, development, documentation, review and control of requirements.

Requirements Traceability Matrix

62. A table that allows each requirement to be traced to those who requested and approved it. Also may match requirements to deliverables, business capabilities and anything else that needs to be traceable.

Residual Risk

63. The risk that remains after risk treatment.

Resource Breakdown Structure

64. A hierarchical depiction of resources by function and type. Makes it clear how each skill and ability fits into a project. Also provides a hierarchy of resources such as materials, equipment and software.

Resource Calendar

65. A calendar of work days available to a project for each resource. Tracks things such as training, vacation and non-project work commitments of a project team.

Resource Leveling

66. A process of resource optimization and resolution of resource conflicts such as a person who is scheduled for two tasks simultaneously. Generally results in changes to the schedule that may impact the critical path and all project dates.

Risk

67. The potential for a negative event or condition to occur that impacts a project. Most project management methodologies currently embrace the idea of positive risk, meaning that a risk can also be the chance of something good happening.

Risk Acceptance

68. One way to treat a risk is simply to formally accept it.

Risk Avoidance

69. Avoiding a risk typically involves changes to project approach or requirements.

Risk Breakdown Structure

70. A hierarchical representation of project risks by category.

Risk Management Plan

71. A document that describes how risks will be managed. Typically includes the Risk Matrix and documentation of risk treatments.

Risk Matrix

72. A table that lists the probability and impact for each identified project risk.

Risk Mitigation

73. Taking actions that reduce the impact or probability of a risk.

Risk Owner

74. The person responsible for treating and monitoring a risk.

Risk Register

75. A repository that documents risk management information such as risks, impacts, probabilities, treatments, triggers and risk owners.

Risk Sharing

76. A risk treatment that distributes a risk in order to improve commitment to a project or improve risk mitigation. In some cases, a project risk will be seen as an opportunity to a particular team or department. For example, a resource risk may be an opportunity to a team that has idle resources.

77. A risk level that's used to make the decision to accept risk. Risks below the threshold are accepted and risks above the threshold are treated.

Risk Tolerance

78. The level of risk that an organization is willing to take on.

Risk Transfer

79. Transfer of project risks to a third party using techniques such as outsourcing.

Schedule

80. The schedule of a project broken down by activity including resources, durations, planned dates and milestones.

Schedule Baseline

81. The approved version of a schedule that is used to evaluate project results.

Schedule Compression

82. An attempt to deliver faster without reducing project scope using techniques such as fast tracking and crashing.

Schedule Variance

83. A measure of performance to schedule commonly defined as the difference between earned value and planned value. In other words, how late or early a project, milestone or phase is delivered.

84. Scope is the work required to complete a project, phase or activity.

Scope Baseline

85. An approved version of a scope statement. Modifications to baseline scope typically require a change request.

Scope Creep

86. Uncontrolled expansion of scope. Expanding scope without making adjustments to time, resources and budget is a common cause of project failure.

Scope Management Plan

87. Defines how scope will be identified, monitored and controlled.

Scope Statement

88. Outlines the work required for a project including assumptions, deliverables and constraints.

Secondary Risk

89. A risk that results from efforts to transfer, share, mitigate or avoid risk. In some cases, efforts to manage risk end up increasing risk. For example, attempting to transfer risks by outsourcing to a partner can result in a variety of partner management risks.

Sponsor

90. The client who owns the project. The sponsor plays a variety of project roles including developing the project charter and project governance functions.

Staffing Management Plan

91. A plan for the acquisition and management of human resources.

Stakeholder

92. An individual, group or organization who affects the project or is affected by the project. Includes everyone who participates in the project or who needs information and notifications from the project.

Stakeholder Management Plan

93. Describes how stakeholders will be engaged in decision making, process execution and communications.

94. According to common project management terminology, a threat is a negative risk. It should be noted that threat has a slightly different meaning in the context of risk management.

Treatment

95. An action that is taken to manage risk.

Trigger Condition

96. An event that causes a risk to occur.

Variance Analysis

97. An analysis of the difference between baseline and actual performance. Usually focused on determining why a project is late or over budget.

98. The degree to which a project meets budget and cost commitments.

Work Breakdown Structure

99. A hierarchy that breaks project work into manageable phases, deliverables and work packages.

Work Package

100. The lowest level of work that is measured and represented in a work breakdown structure.

Workaround

101. A tactical action that overcomes a project issue or removes an obstacle.

16 Types of Project Stakeholder

A stakeholder is any individual, team or organization that is affected by a project. These include both working members who are accountable or responsible for aspects of a project and stakeholders who are simply consulted or informed. The following are a few common types of stakeholders:

1. Project Sponsor

The persons accountable and responsible for representing the sponsoring business.

2. Customer or Client

Representatives from the sponsoring business who have a stake or role in the project such as providing requirements.

3. Program Management

A project may fall under a program or impact programs.

4. Project Management

Managers of the project or projects that are related or impacted.

5. Business Analysts

Business analysts deliver artifacts such as the project's business case or requirements.

6. Project Team

Generally defined as anyone who contributes work to the project.

7. Project Management Office

An organization's Project Management Office may have interest in project in order to monitor a project portfolio or maintain project management standards.

8. Project Management Board

Project governance bodies such as a Project Management Board.

9. Executive Team

Generally a project wants to garner as much executive attention as possible in order to create visibility that helps to clear issues and recognize project successes.

10. Functional Managers

Managers who are impacted by business change driven by a project or who have resources committed to the project.

11. Architects & Designers

Members of the project team who are responsible for delivering aspects of the project's architecture and design.

12. Internal Stakeholders

A term for stakeholders who work for the client organization.

13. External Stakeholders

A term for anyone involved in a project who doesn't work for the client organization such as contractors, vendors, partners and suppliers.

14. End Customers

The customers of the project's sponsoring business unit.

15. Local Communities

In many cases, members of the local community have stake in a project. For example, the neighbors of a large construction site may be impacted and compensated for disruption to their use or enjoyment of their property. In such cases, they may be informed of project schedule updates.

16. Regulators

Some projects attract the interest of government agencies who become stakeholders. In many cases, government approvals are a project dependency.

19 Agile Principles

Agile is a project methodology that began as a short statement of 12 software development principles entitled Manifesto for Agile Software Development published by a group of 17 prominent software developers in 2001.

The principles had a profound effect on software development as a dozen or more agile methodologies sprang from them. With time, several other widely accepted principles have arguably evolved. The following principles are commonly associated with agile methodologies.

Continuous Delivery

1. Agile frequently delivers.

Change

2. Change is accepted at any time.

Working Software

3. Delivery is measured in working software.

4. Delivery cycles can be counted in weeks not months.

Integrated Teams

5. Teams include business and technical members. Everyone you need to deliver is on the team.

Trust

6. Teams are trusted.

7. Agile only works with motivated, high performance teams.

Face To Face

8. A team sits close together and face-to-face communication is preferred.

Sustainable Pace

9. Work is at a sustainable pace that can be continued indefinitely.

Good Design

10. Teams prioritize good design.

11. Defined in the original manifesto as the "art of maximizing the amount of work not done."

Self Organizing Teams

12. Teams are allowed to self-organize without management interference.

Roles

13. Teams may have different roles but these are kept as general as possible.

14. Teams take time to reflect on recent performance to identify improvements.

15. Agile teams have a tendency to timebox meetings and delivery cycles.

Continuous Integration

16. Work is continuously integrated into a single releasable product.

Small Teams

17. Agile teams tend to be small and this is often considered of importance.

Last Responsible Moment

18. No big upfront plan, architecture or design.

Method Tailoring

19. Agile encourages teams to customize methodologies and develop a strong team culture.

26 Scrum Basics

Scrum is an agile technique of project delivery that uses quick iterations that build working features that are potentially shippable. It is based on a set of conventions and unique language for things that could have used more common terms. This is intentional as scrum is designed to leave the old ways of project management behind. Scrum also depends on the unique culture that has evolved around it. Teams are encouraged to customize it, stress it and improve it. As a result, scrum has a slightly different flavor from one team to the next. The following are common scrum conventions.

A comprehensive list of user expectations for each user story that serve as detailed functional requirements.

1. Acceptance Testing

Acceptance testing is functional testing of the acceptance criteria in user stories. Also known as User Acceptance Testing, or UAT.

2. Backlog Refinement

Backlog refinement is the practice of improving product backlog items. For example, acceptance criteria may be added to user stories. Product backlog items may also be dropped if they are no longer needed.

3. Burndown Chart

A graphical representation of work remaining vs time that can be created for an epic, version or sprint.

4. Daily Scrum

A quick meeting held each day of a sprint that has a particular set of conventions. Each contributing member of a scrum team reports what they did yesterday, what they will do today and any impediments that are in their way.

5. Definition Of Done

Definition of Done is a set of completion criteria that a scrum team adopts to set expectations for what it means for a feature to be "done"

6. Epics

A big user story that is too big to implement directly but instead acts as a campaign that might include hundreds of user stories.

7. Feature

A feature is a general term for an epic, theme, user story or technical requirement.

8. Impediments

An impediment is any issue or problem that is preventing the completion of a feature that requires the attention of the scrum team.

9. Potentially Shippable

The features delivered by each sprint are potentially shippable. This indicates they can be launched if a business unit decides they're ready. The definition of done that each team adopts defines what it means for a feature to be potentially shippable.

10. Product Backlog

A product backlog is a prioritized list of user stories, technical requirements, bugs and knowledge acquisition activities associated with a particular product. It is normal for a product backlog to grow reasonably large as a pool of ideas for improving a product. In sprint planning, teams decide which items to move from the product backlog to the sprint backlog for the next sprint.

11. Product Owner
A single person who has authority to represent the customer on a scrum team. The product owner is responsible for the backlog, prioritization and clarifications of requirements. As scrum teams are self-organizing, the product owner has no particular authority over the team, despite representing the sponsoring business unit.

12. Release
Releasing the product to the customer. Each sprint ends with a potentially shippable product version. The product owner decides if the release is made by considering its value to customers against costs and risks.

13. Scrum Of Scrums
A meeting to coordinate the efforts of multiple scrum teams. Scrum teams are best kept small and scrum is scaled using multiple teams. As such, the scrum of scrums is the primary means of achieving scrum scale.

14. Scrum Team
Scrum teams are small with less than a dozen members or so. Roles on the team are kept as general as possible. For example, a scrum team might include a scrummaster, product owner and 4-6 developers.

15. Scrummaster
A scrummaster is a facilitator who coordinates the scrum team and owns the scrum process. It is specifically not a management role. The scrummaster makes sure the team lives up to the values and practices of scrum. For example, a scrummaster coaches members of the team in scrum and makes sure that the relationship between the product owner and the rest of the team is productive.

16. Spike
A term for activities such as research and prototyping that doesn't directly change the product.

17. Sprint
A sprint is the scrum development cycle. It is a short timeboxed effort of 1-4 weeks that delivers working code that is potentially shippable.

18. Sprint Backlog
A sprint backlog is a list of items to be completed on a sprint. Items may include user stories, bugs, non-functional requirements, knowledge acquisition and prototypes.

19. Sprint Goal
A short statement that gives a mission or theme to a sprint. In many cases, they are simply a descriptive summary of the sprint backlog.

20. Sprint Planning
A timeboxed meeting that plans a sprint. Involves clarifying items, developing estimates, prioritizing, moving items from the product backlog to the spring backlog and creating a sprint goal.

21. Sprint Retrospective
A short meeting to review a sprint and identify improvements.

22. Sprint Task
Tasks are things that need to be done to complete an item on the sprint backlog. They are typically tracked on a board with the headings to do, in process and done for each user story.

23. Theme
A theme is a label that is applied to a group of stories to indicate their context such as a particular business strategy.

24. User Stories
A type of functional requirement that's stated from a user perspective.

25. Velocity
The amount of work that a team can complete in a sprint. Typically measured by recent results in story points.

15 Immutable Laws of Project Management

LAW 1: No major project is ever completed on time, within budget, with the same staff that started it, nor does the project do what it is supposed to do. It is highly unlikely that yours will be the first.

Corollary 1: The benefits will be smaller than initially estimated, if estimates were made at all.

Corollary 2: The system finally installed will be completed late and will not do what it is supposed to do.

Corollary 3: It will cost more but will be technically successful.

LAW 2: One advantage of fuzzy project objectives is that they let you avoid embarrassment in estimating the corresponding costs.

LAW 3: The effort required to correct a project that is off course increases geometrically with time.

Corollary 1: The longer you wait the harder it gets.

Corollary 2: If you wait until the project is completed, its too late.

Corollary 3: Do it now regardless of the embarrassment.

LAW 4: The project purpose statement you wrote and understand will be seen differently by everyone else.

Corollary 1: If you explain the purpose so clearly that no one could possibly misunderstand, someone will.

Corollary 2: If you do something that you are sure will meet everyone's approval, someone will not like it.

LAW 5: Measurable benefits are real. Intangible benefits are not measurable, thus intangible benefits are not real.

Corollary 1: Intangible benefits are real if you can prove that they are real.

LAW 6: Anyone who can work effectively on a project part-time certainly does not have enough to do now.

Corollary 1: If a boss will not give a worker a full-time job, you shouldn't either.

Corollary 2: If the project participant has a time conflict, the work given by the full-time boss will not suffer.

LAW 7: The greater the project's technical complexity, the less you need a technician to manage it.

Corollary 1: Get the best manager you can. The manager will get the technicians.

Corollary 2: The reverse of corollary 1 is almost never true.

LAW 8: A carelessly planned project will take three times longer to complete than expected. A carefully planned project will only take twice as long.

Corollary 1: If nothing can possibly go wrong, it will anyway.

LAW 9: When the project is going well, something will go wrong.

Corollary 1: When things cannot get any worse, they will.

Corollary 2: When things appear to be going better, you have overlooked something.

LAW 10: Project teams detest weekly progress reporting because it so vividly manifests their lack of progress.

LAW 11: Projects progress rapidly until they are 90 percent complete. Then they remain 90 percent complete forever.

LAW 12: If project content is allowed to change freely, the rate of change will exceed the rate of progress.

LAW 13: If the user does not believe in the system, a parallel system will be developed. Neither system will work very well.

LAW 14: Benefits achieved are a function of the thoroughness of the post-audit check.

Corollary 1: The prospect of an independent post-audit provides the project team with a powerful incentive to deliver a good system on schedule within budget.

LAW 15: No law is immutable.

10 Project Management Best Practices

When you're studying project management, you'll probably experience a few of these moments: "Ooh, that's a good point! I should remember that advice." Only to forget a few weeks later.

If you're wrapped up in practicing the big-picture principles of project management, it's easy to forget the little details that make the best project managers worth emulating.

1. Communicate with all project stakeholders

From the first day you kick the project off you need to be communicating. Not to just a select few, but to all the project stakeholders. This includes key people like team members, managers, project sponsors, clients, and valued users.

2. Create a risk response team

Projects and tasks are all subject to different levels of risk. That's why you should always have a risk response team. They can help a project remain in the green and avoid going in the yellow... or the dreaded red. Think of a risk response team as the first line of defense when problems occur.

3. Hold a project kick-off

In order to manage a successful project, you need to align all your stakeholders with an initial kick-off meeting. You should include everyone that is going to have a stake in the project, so that way expectations are managed up front. The earlier you get on their radar the better. This will help with communicating smaller tasks and assignments to various team members down the line. Making sure everyone is aware of the project from the beginning is a simple, yet effective way to drive a healthy project to production.

4. Use a detailed work definition document

A common issue with managing projects is clarifying who is responsible for what. A detailed work document takes care of the uncertainty and confusion. It clearly documents what level of work needs to be done by what group or individual, so everyone has a clear understanding of the level of effort involved. To create accountability within your project, use a detailed work definition document and make all your stakeholders sign in agreement.

5. Create a detailed work plan

Formalizing your project's work plan is key to meeting deadlines and hitting milestones. Without a detailed work plan, there isn't a documented plan for all the various stages of the project. What gets measured gets done, and a detailed work plan is a simple way to measure all the different moving parts of a project.

6. Document everything

As a project manager, have you ever seen an assignment slip by a few days, or worse, a few weeks? Why did this happen? What caused this to happen? How do we prevent it from happening again?

In order to answer these questions, you need to draw on evidence. Documenting everything that happens in your project is a sure-fire way to ensure sure you have all the data you need to make better decisions and learn from previous challenges. So write everything down! Project steps, bottlenecks, scope changes, task dependencies. Even having stakeholder PTO times accounted for come in handy.

7. Ask for feedback

None of us are perfect, and there will be good and bad every step of the way, even regarding the project manager's performance. Being aware of personal room for an improvement is an extremely powerful tool to harness. Especially if you are willing to take criticism from your team.

As a project manager, your job is to ensure the success of

the project. And remember that humans are at the other end of the project assignment. Asking for feedback is a great way to increase the chances of success and better your management skills.

8. Communicate the impact of project add-ons

It's easy to say "Yes" to every new project or task that comes up. However, this is a good way of getting yourself into project overload. Anytime you have a new request within your project, it's your responsibility to show how this will affect your timeline or budget.

9. Manage new agreements

New requests often mean a change in original project scope. If this happens, then it's a best practice to have everyone sign a new agreement document. This will give the various stakeholders a clear understanding of the new scope of work and what the impact is to the overall project. It also creates a documented agreement, so there is minimal confusion if deadlines need to be moved.

10. Hold a wrap-up meeting

Once your project has been completed, it's time to reflect and see how you can optimize the next projects for success. Holding a wrap-up meeting is a perfect opportunity to get all of the project members together for discussion. Go over lessons learned and ways to improve for next time. Following a similar or the exact same flawed process over and over won't help you succeed. Continuously optimizing your work management will go a long way in saving you time and money.

63 Experts Share Their #1 Tip

We asked experienced project managers to divulge their #1 tip for newcomers to the field. Not surprisingly, these process fanatics shared a plethora of great tips to help newcomers succeed in this ever-changing area of work.

Read through their project management advice below, and see what you can learn as you walk into your first, second, or even tenth PM role.

"I think that all the important tips could be summarized with a metaphor:
You should be like an Orchestra Director for your team, with a detailed project plan as score."
— Jose Ignacio Bernaldo de Quiros Ochoa

Everyone Agrees — Excellent Communication is the #1 Indicator of Success

1. Understand the culture

Communication is key, and much of that will be informal, so building your network and understanding culture and dynamics are key.
Thomas J. Dickie, PMP

2. Be accessible to learn more

Always allow people to come to you. Be accessible and listen to what project team members will ask

or comment all the time. The more you know, the better you are able to make decisions. Buy knowledge and sell solutions unless you want to pay for project deviations.
Fábio Issao Watanabe

3. Communicate to identify changes quickly

I think that success depends on communication and focus on the goal. Good communication with the team identifies deviations in a timely manner. Good communication with customers can quickly identify changes in scope.
Oscar Teran

4. Keep detailed project notes to share

Follow up on tasks and Communicate, Communicate, Communicate. Keep detailed notes and make sure everyone on the team is aware of what is happening.
Monteau (Montee) Outlaw

5. Discuss challenges, roadblocks, & risks

Make sure to be transparent within your core and your extended project team, as well towards your managers, owner, sponsor. Communicate roadblocks, challenges, and risks clearly and in advance for everyone to see. Know and accept: no one cares for, or is as committed to your project as much, as you are/must be.
Janos Veres

6. Listen to opinions from everyone, even if you reject them later

Keep communication channels open for all stakeholders: the team, the sponsor, the customer, the end user, your boss, etc. I am not saying that you let yourself be manipulated by every party, just try to listen before making decisions. Hear every opinion, then make your route.

Mehmet Degirmencioglu

7. Respect every opinion as if it were your own

Train communication, create empathy with your stakeholders. Respect and value everybody's opinions, even if you don't completely agree.

João Rodrigues

8. Challenge ideas to make them better

You are hired to manage projects; your team is hired to be the technical expertise to deliver that project. Therefore, if they are telling you something, it's usually a good idea to take in what they're saying and, in some cases, challenge it. If you're not technical, ask for clarification on points you genuinely don't understand. That's normally enough for technical teams to make them think through their explanations, so they'll carry out an internal check to ensure their thinking is sound.

Andrew Hudson

9. Build rapport and trust with clients

Build rapport with the client. Build trust and then never lose it. Under promise and over deliver. Plan and communicate.

Marc Hammoud

10. Don't Pretend You Know Everything on Day One Always ask "that question"

You may not have the experience needed to do things 100% correct the first time, so keep it real and allow people to give you suggestions. My #1 suggestion to newbies is: Always ask "that question". Finding a balance between asking questions or following up offline is a talent you will learn over time, but for now, don't be shy. You might harm your own project by not speaking up until it becomes a show stopper near implementation time. Speak up and you will find your team is truly on your side!

John Skowronski, PMI-ACP, PM

11. Don't isolate your team with overconfidence

Do not think you know everything. I've seen too many project managers take a hard line and push things through because they think they know best. That breeds resentment in the project team. I've seen project managers exert their supposed technical or subject authority on a project, only for that project to ultimately remove those additions at a later and more expensive stage.

Andrew Hudson

12. Learn from every experience

You don't have to know everything about everything — it's ok to ask questions and learn from each experience.

Ann Lynne Dodson

13. To Be the Best, Hone Your Leadership & Management Skills. Make sure you motivate and lead your team

Soft skills are very important. The people involved make the difference between success and failure. You can have knowledge and methods, but you need skills to motivate and lead.

Maarten Verreck

14. Manage your people, not just your documentation

Following the PM process and keeping up with all the communication tools like the risk log, issue log, schedule, and deliverables should all take a back seat to leading your team. For years I prided myself in being really good at the documentation side of project management, but it never really mattered that much. The most important skill a project manager must master is Leadership!

Larry Sparkman

15. Build a bridge for two-way trust

Trust is the biggest thing for me, because if I don't trust my technical team then I'm inherently suspicious of them and vice versa. Building a relationship of trust, and therefore openness, is crucial if you are to deliver multiple successful projects.

Andrew Hudson

16. Stay flexible to take on every challenge

Keep your knowledge constantly updated, trying to develop new capabilities and remaining flexible in terms of project management methodologies to use, etc. Things can change very rapidly in this field, and as the leader of your team, flexibility and a listening ear are most important to manage the risks and change.   Nirmal Singh

17. Delegate wisely and lead by example

Learn what you can delegate. Learn who you can delegate to. Lead by example. Work harder than anyone else. Treat everyone you touch with respect and kindness.

Lori Galster

18. Train your people to be future leaders

It should always be remembered that delegation is not purely about sharing workload. Also it gives the team member a sense of ownership and liability and allows them to learn... Today's team member can be tomorrow's PM.

Andy Nelson, AMBCS, P2 Cert Practitioner

19. Think outside the box

The key for successful PM is communication, problem-solving, and decision-making. Working smarter and offering solutions. Thinking outside the box and strategically looking at the bigger picture.

Kassim Toorawa

20. Protect your team

You "Protect" the project team, they do the rest.

Onur Karabulut

21. And don't forget to proactively celebrate success!

The most important part: celebrate with your team who made it possible!

Puneet Gulati, MSP, PMP, ITIL v3

22. Be the Person Who Keeps Work Organized & Meetings Focused

23. Use templates to stay organized
Try to stay as organized as you can, use templates and other tools provided by PMI (you can find them on PMI's website).
Bhawna Mundotia, PMP

24. Document! Document! Document!
Always keep a track record of the work being done.
Pietro Cecere

25. Step up and capture ideas during meetings
If you are in a meeting that needs focus because people are talking in circles, step up to the white board or large note pad and start scribing their ideas, requirements, comments, issues, etc. — preferably into actionable categories. Do not speak! Just scribe. If they start to focus on what you are writing, then you can ask them if they want to identify owners for each actionable item.
Jerry B. Fisher

26. Learn What Inspires Your New Team, Then Achieve Success Together
Know the working culture before you introduce change. First understand the work/culture/situation, and then make your moves/changes. PMs always want to do something new and different based on their experiences, which is a good thing,

but do it smartly. You can't just jump in and start making changes to the system without understanding it; every company has their own limitations, constraints, and culture. Make changes in such a way that they get absorbed in the right attitude.
Santosh Maurya

27. Understand everyone's motivations

Learn that project management can be as much about politics as handling projects. Remember that not everyone working on the project is actually for the project. Learn the motivations and intentions of not just your team, but also upwards to the stakeholders and business users.
Andy Nelson, AMBCS, P2 Cert Practitioner

28. Build a culture of sharing and innovation to build a strong team

Foster a culture where everyone's ideas are heard to allow more innovation to take place. The added bonus is that the project team itself becomes a lot stronger — team members are far more open to suggesting and working through ideas if they know they'll be heard, rather than thinking they'll be shouted down all the time.
Andrew Hudson

29. Know the Limitations of Your Project Team — And Yourself. Don't forget the human

The methodologies are great if well-used, but they won't work if you do not remember that you are working with other people. Human responses are not always logical or predictable.

Tiago Prado

30. Know your team's strengths

Understand the skill set & mind set of the people that you're going to handle in your team.

Prabhu M

31. Leave egos behind
Be aware of strengths and limitations in your team and, more importantly, yourself. There is no room for egos.

Louie Turcotte, Jr

32. Find what sets you apart

Determine your specialization and go for it. The best thing you can do is to decide what sets you apart and make that shine. Remember you are turning concepts into realities and it takes creativity to get you there. Develop thick skin and never fall in love with your first draft, no matter what it is.

James L Thompson, PMP, CSM, Executive MBA, ITIL

33. Ask Questions to Understand Current Processes, & Keep Them Simple

34. Ask follow-up questions
When someone makes a suggestion, I like to follow up with background questions: When and under what circumstances have you implemented that in the past? Why was that approach successful? What made it more efficient, cost effective, etc.? Then I broaden my scope of understanding.
Lori Galster

35. Don't make mountains out of molehills
DON'T make a huge mind-numbing deal out of the project. Newbies are generally so eager to implement their knowledge or are so psyched up about being in the shoes of a PM, they generally end up overcomplicating simple things. I have seen "accidental" project managers perform better than those who come to the job armed with the whole pedigree of PM tools, techniques, and strategies. It's better to keep work simple and streamlined so that attention can be devoted to planning, actual implementation, and overall scope and quality control, instead of waiting for the heavens to open up and rain down!
Trina Moitra

36. Make progress the priority

Do not always look at things from a process perspective. Governance is important, but when it impedes progress then there is an issue.

Dave Regan

37. Clarify Everyone's Roles & Responsibilities on Every Project

Understand your own role first

Clearly understand your role and responsibilities and your delegated authority. This will depend on the type of organization you're operating under. Also understand your key stakeholders and their level of influence.

Kassim Toorawa

38. Analyze project heartbeats daily

I suggest accidental managers follow the RACI model and analyze project heartbeats daily.

R- Who is Responsible to do the work

A- Who is Accountable for final decisions and ultimate ownership

B- Who is Consulted before a decision or action is taken

— *Who is Informed that the decision or action has been taken*

39. The RACI model is helpful to define/identify/clarify roles and responsibilities

Once you have those, match them up with processes. It's especially useful in clarifying roles and responsibilities in cross-functional processes. For example, an organization may have a person who performs the role of project manager, and may also perform the role of test manager.

Hambirrao_Patil

40. Beware of role creep

Watch for ROLE creep, which is similar to scope creep in a project. In role creep, your role as a PM might be under constant pressure — from academics, LinkedIn groups, co-workers, and especially those working above you. This is because there are so many forces at work around a substantial project, especially in a non-projectized organization where there is no discipline to comply with standardized and repeatable project management processes. There will be pressure to be innovative, be creative, and be an agent of change, and you will have managers asking you to list all your accomplishments. Your ultimate role is always to deliver what is in the WBS and project plan, use a designated process for scope change, risk monitoring, and issue management, and maintain good communication.

Michael Ayres MS, PMP, CISSP, CSEP

41. Make Sure You Have a Full Understanding of the Project Objectives, Assets, & Risks. Know the project inside out

Understand the project — so the planning, objectives, results that the project wants to achieve, and of course know the monitoring plan: what are the indicators, its tools, etc.

Marta Acero

42. Set the goals first

Establish the goal and objectives (SMART) of your new project. Once this is done well, I would immediately do the PESTEL analysis and build the SWOT analysis. Then, it's planning, communication, and organization. For your project setup plan, you can also use the What, When, Who, Which, Where, etc. model.

Osvaldo Mirante, PhD

43. Understand the project needs

Having a clear understanding of both the functional and technical definition/needs of the project upfront, with stakeholder buy-in, is extremely important.

Muqtader MBA

44. Make sure the project achieves its original goal

Focus on specified project objectives!
Muqtader MBA

45. Control the project scope

Knowing your exact scope of work very well is the key to controlling the rest.
Mohammad Hamdan, PMP®

46. Think about what can outside forces could affect your project — positively or negatively

Look for organizational process assets that are available to you. Identify the environmental factors that will influence your projects and how they'll be delivered.
Thomas J. Dickie, PMP

47. Make work actionable

Make sure everything is actionable and responsibilities are assigned and transparent.
Henriette Ebbesen Laidlaw

48. Allow time for multiple iterations

Plan and drive project activities according to strategic guidelines. Allow the project team a few iterations over viable and plausibly valid alternative solutions. Never be afraid to ask the project owner for clarification or adjustment of target, timeline, resources, or scope.

Janos Veres

49. Don't forget to manage potential risks

You need to understand the organization's culture to make a roadmap and deliver projects on time and within budget. You should also keep an eye on risks arising during the course of project implementation, with a risk mitigation plan in place.

Puneet Gulati, MSP, PMP, ITIL v3

50. Get Buy-In From Stakeholders Early & Manage Their Expectations Along the Way. Identify every stakeholder

Identify all stakeholders and develop terms of references. This will align all roles of different individuals in the project and make it easier to relate with them.

Lesiba Noah Konaite

51. Sell the project to all necessary parties

Involve as many as possible stakeholders at the beginning of a project to gain broader buy-in.
Andries Venter, Inclusive Project Manager

52. Hold 1-on-1 project feedback sessions

Before kicking off the project, connect with all the key stakeholders in 1-on-1 sessions to get their input on the project, their goals, their level of support, etc. This will uncover hidden "gotchas" and misalignment that may come up later if you don't do this.
Tom Treanor

53. Make stakeholders believe in the goal, not just the budget

Getting stakeholder buy-in on the outcome and benefit of completing the project is more important than stakeholder acceptance of the scope, schedule, and budget. If decision-makers believe in what the project will achieve, they will be more likely to accept changes to the scope and tolerances if you can show that it will lead to a better outcome. If all you've sold is a budget and a delivery date, you're doomed to failure.
Chris Cox

54. Continually manage expectations as the project goes on

Manage the stakeholders' expectations within given limits. That would encompass all the necessary requirements such as deliverables, scope, etc.

John Mpungu

55. Don't Be Afraid of Failure, Learn From It. Fail fast, recover faster

Failure is an option. Fail fast so you can recover quickly and learn.

Sreekumar Govindan

56. Turn mistakes into learning opportunities

Don't be afraid of mistakes — learn from them. They are the building blocks for future success in this challenging and dynamic profession!

Susan Kirkpatrick, PMP, CSSBB

57. Deliver what the business actually needs

A high percentage of projects fail because they don't deliver what the business needs. Even when you have that nice 400-page requirements document that was signed off on, it does not mean everyone understands what is being delivered.

Thomas J. Dickie, PMP

58. Ultimate Success Comes From Careful Management, Not Just Careful Planning
Manage the problem, not just the Gantt chart

Reality drives the schedule, not the other way around. It's not about wrangling Gantt charts, it's about wrangling people and problems.

James Radvan

59. Plan to succeed & persevere

Every day there is a chance that you will have your back to the wall. Plan to succeed. Coordinate your priorities, delegate to those in your team, and make the project work.

Paul Alwood

60. Keep your eye on the overall objectives

No one on the business side cares about the Gantt chart or status reports or the PM deliverables. What they are looking for is the capabilities to achieve the business objectives your project will deliver.

Thomas J. Dickie, PMP

61. And Remember: Nothing Beats Hands-On Experience

You can't fake experience. Experience is the most valued ingredient of the perfect PM brew, and that can either come with the salt and pepper of years

or from a very competent mentor. There is no way to fake experience.
Trina Moitra

62. Expose yourself to real-life situations early on

Gain as much experience in project management as you can. Books, theory, and concepts are all fine, but real-life situations are much tougher. The more you face these situations, the smarter you become. There is no better way to learn project management than to expose yourself to real-life situations.
Mangal Pandya

63. Rely on your people skills, and push for the success at the end of the project

Don't give up. A Project Manager position is not a rewarding job every day. You have to work really hard to get things done (especially in a Matrix environment), so you have to rely on your people skills a lot. (Keep those sharp!) In the end, you will persevere, and when the project finishes successfully, you will love that feeling of success.
Bhawna Mundotia, PMP

8 Reasons, Benefits and Overviews

Benefits of Project Management

80% of "high-performing" projects are led by a certified project manager.

ROI of project managers (including average salary and training costs):

Entry level   501% ROI

Mid-level   268% ROI

Senior level   358% ROI

89% of high-performing organizations value project management,

81% actively engage sponsors,

57% align projects with business strategy.

46% of organizations admit to not fully understanding the value of project management, even though that understanding boosts the success rate of strategic initiatives by 16%.

1. Project Management Methodologies

59% say either most departments or their entire organization uses standard project management practices.

Organizations that use a methodology:

38% meet budget

28% stay on schedule

71% meet scope

68% meet quality standards

60% meet expected benefits

VS.

Organizations that don't use a methodology:

31% meet budget

21% stay on schedule

61% meet scope

60% meet quality standards

51% meet expected benefits

Popular Methodologies:

41% use PMBoK

26% do not use a standard methodology

9% use an IT methodology

9% use another approach

8% use a combination of methods

4% use an in-house method to manage projects

3% use PRINCE2

2. Project Management Best Practices

Having a knowledge transfer process in place boosts the chance of project success by over 20%.

More than 90% of organizations perform some type of project postmortem or closeout retrospective. [9]

64% of organizations say they frequently conduct risk management.

30% of project managers break up large projects into smaller segments, with deliverables and evaluations at the end of each segment.

How Project Success is Measured:

20% — Satisfied stakeholders

19% — Delivered on time

18% — Delivered within budget

17% — Achieves target benefits

15% — Produces high-quality deliverables

9% — Achieves acceptable ROI

2% — Other

Keys to Project Success:

48% say the team's technical skills

41% say executive support

26% say effective team communication

19% say Agile techniques

17% say the leadership of certified Project Managers

12% say effective soft skills among staff

3. Agile Project Management

38% of organizations report using agile frequently.

75% of highly agile organizations met their goals/business intent,

65% finished on time,

and 67% finished within budget.

Compared to organizations with low agility, where only 56% met their business goals, 40% finished on time, and 45% finished within budget.

Agile organizations successfully complete more of their strategic initiatives than less agile organizations. (69% to 45%).

Agile organizations grow revenue 37% faster and generate 30% higher profits than non-agile companies.

Most Popular Agile Tools and Processes:

Scrum – 43%

Lean & Test Driven Development (TDD) – 11%

eXtreme Programming – 10%

Feature Development Driven – 9%

Complex Adaptive System – 4%

Crystal – 3%

Dynamic Systems Development Method – 3%

Other – 6%

None – 10%

5. Project Management Salaries

Average Project Manager Salaries:

Entry-level	$54,953
Managing small, low-risk projects	$65,818
Managing medium-size, moderate-risk projects	$81,520
Managing large, highly integrated projects	$103,047

On average, it takes 7 years in the profession to go from entry-level to managing large, complex projects.

Average Salary of Senior-Level PM by Region:

Southwest US	$108,300
Southeast US	$98,864
Midwest US	$97,778
Mid-Atlantic US	$110,096
Northwest US	$101,446
Northeast US	$103,511
Outside US	$108,300

Average Salary of Senior-Level PM by Industry:

Energy/Utilities	$147,600
Aerospace/Defense	$116,100
Government – Federal	$113,000
Information/Technology	$107,200
Construction/Engineering	$104,800
Financial Services	$104,500
Telecommu-Nications	$102,800
Pharma/Healthcare	$101,800
Automotive/Manufacturing	$99,760
Management Consulting	$100,700
Media	$94,340
Government – City/State/Local	$90,080
NonProfit/Education	$72,920

According to respondents, five days per year of project-focused training reduced the amount of time it took to advance from an entry-level project manager to a senior project manager by 12.6 months.

Project Management Professional (PMP)® certified project managers in the U.S. earned an average of 16% more (approximately $14,500) than their non-credentialed peers in 2011.

3. Project Management Training & Certification

61% of project management practitioners say their organization currently offers ongoing project management training for staff.

PM Certification by Department:

37% say their entire IT department is certified.

33% say IT department managers are certified.

26% say Business managers are certified.

25% say Business staff is certified (both managers and non-managers).

10% say Executive managers are certified.

29% say no one on staff is certified.

Types of Project Management Training Offered by Organizations:

Classroom setting – 28%

Online self-paced course – 24%

Online situational sessions – 18%

Paper-based self-studies – 16%

All of the above – 13%

Other – 1%

Number of PMI Certified Project Managers:

Total Number of PMP credential holders: 607,128

# of CAPM certification holders: 25,060

Program Management Professional credential holders: 1,027

PMI Agile Certified Practitioner holders: 5,265

4. Project Management Software & Tools

77% of companies use project management software, and 87% of high-performing companies use project management software.

Top Business Challenges that Lead People to Project Management Software:

Capturing time/cost of projects: 62%

Approvals are paper-based: 55%

Re-entering lost data: 45%

Lack of integration between tools: 38%

No central source of project information: 35%

Poor visibility & resource management: 31%

Poor purchasing processes: 23%

Lack of visibility into work in progress: 21%

Most-Wanted Features in Project Management Software:

1. Reliability

2. Ease of integration

3. Ease of use

66% said they choose a project management software based on level of support available.

Popular Tools for Managing IT Projects:

70% use status reports

68% use the project plan documentation

63% use spreadsheets

53% use project management software

45% use help desk tickets, work orders, or a task tracking system

36% use time reporting at the project level

31% use communication templates

25% use quality assessments

21% use real-time status dashboards

20% use a homegrown/in-house solution

18% use word processing documents

10% use earned value management reports

The most important factor in choosing which software to purchase was functionality (40%), followed by ease of use (24%).

Most-used features include file sharing, time tracking, email integration, and Gantt charts.

Business aspects significantly improved by PM software:

Team communication – 52%

Quality of final product – 44%

Number of projects completed on budget – 44%

Number of projects completed on time – 44%

Customer satisfaction – 38%

66% of organizations use PM software to communicate with clients. [17]

76% of respondents said they are either "very satisfied" or "satisfied" with their PM software.

5. Project Management Industry Growth

Between 2010 and 2020, 15.7 million new project management roles will be created globally, and the project management industry is slated to grow by $6.61 trillion.

An expected 12% growth in demand for project management professionals will result in almost 6.2 million jobs by 2020.

Business services (2 million jobs) and Manufacturing (630,000 jobs) supported the greatest number of project management roles in 2010. Business services and healthcare are expected to lead job growth between 2010 and 2020.

The healthcare industry is projected to increase project management roles by 30% — a higher growth rate than any current project intensive industry.

Estimated Project-Oriented Job Openings 2010-2020:

China	8,153,340
India	3,975,650
US	2,348,830
Japan	387,560
Brazil	347,820
UK	177,120
Germany	153,230
Canada	120,070
Australia	74,900
United Arab Emirates	18,000
Saudi Arabia	12,670

83% of project organizations reported that they were understaffed at some level. 44% of the reported shortages were for senior-level project managers. 89.4% report that it is either very difficult or somewhat difficult to find senior-level talent.

6. IT Project Management Challenges

The average large IT project runs 45% over budget, 7% over time, and delivers 56% less value than expected.

One in six IT projects has an average cost overrun of 200% and a schedule overrun of 70%.

Nearly 45% admit they're unclear on the business objectives of their IT projects.

Only 34% of respondents say IT projects almost always deliver value to the business. 21% say they sometimes deliver value, and 41% say results are mixed.

78% said their project requirements are usually or always out of sync with the business.

75% of IT project leaders believe their projects are "doomed from the start."

17% of large IT projects (budgets $15M+) go so badly they threaten the existence of the company.

Top Contributors to Large IT Project Failure:

Unclear objectives/lack of business focus

Unrealistic schedule/reactive planning

Shifting requirements/technical complexity

Unaligned team/missing skills

Unexplained causes

Only 47% say their teams achieve 70-89% of their goals. Nearly 20% say they only achieve 50-69% of their goals.

80% of teams say they spend at least half their time reworking completed tasks.

Barriers to Success:

38% cite confusion around team roles and responsibilities.

31% point to being unclear or disagreeing on what constitutes project success.

77% say they don't always agree on when a project is done, leaving the door open for ongoing rework and scope creep.

7. Portfolio Project Management and Project Management Offices

Portfolio Project Management (PPM)

53% of respondents say they have a project portfolio management process in place.

The number of firms with a PPM process in place grew from 64% in 2003 to 71% in 2013.

Popularity by Industry:

Finance – 87%

Healthcare – 76%

Retail/Consumer – 72%

Insurance – 71%

Information/Technology – 67%

Manufacturing – 66%

Automotive – 65%

Banking & Capital Marketing – 60%

Telecommunications – 55%

Energy – 52%

Defense – 51%

Construction – 34%

Other – 51%

26% of firms say they get a 25% or greater ROI from implementing PPM processes.

How Companies Prioritize Projects:

18% say strategic alignment

14% say expected benefits

14% say ROI

Top 5 PPM Functions:

Portfolio tracking & performance monitoring – 75%

Portfolio oversight – 68%

Portfolio planning, resource allocation, and schedule – 66%

Portfolio analysis, project selection, & prioritization – 65%

PPM process implementation & management – 61%

Top 5 PPM Priorities:

Improve resource planning & forecasting – 65%

Implement/enhance reporting, analytics, & dashboard tools – 62%

Implement/enhance PPM processes – 53%

Implement demand management/capacity planning processes – 42%

Implement/enhance performance measurement process – 39%

Top 5 PPM Challenges:

Organization has silo mentality 49%

Consistent application of defined processes – 44%

Getting reliable/accurate project info – 42%

Lack of info on resources- 40%

Inadequate PPM skills- 39%

42% of portfolios are comprised of more than 100 projects, while 25% of portfolios have fewer than 20 projects. [4]

55% of organizations surveyed review project portfolios monthly, 23% review them quarterly.

Project Management Offices (PMOs)

PMO Popularity by Company Size:

61% of small organizations (<$100M) have a PMO

88% of mid-size companies ($100M-$1B) have a PMO

90% of large enterprises (>$1B) have a PMO

Number of companies with a PMO has grown from 47% to 80% from 2000-2012. 30% of companies currently without a PMO plan to start one in the coming year.

PMO Popularity by Industry:

Healthcare – 93%

Finance – 93%

Information Technology – 85%

Manufacturing – 78%

Professional Services – 60%

Benefits of High-Performing PMOs:

45% more projects aligned with business objectives

28% increase in # of projects delivered under budget

$101,000 cost savings per project

27% decrease in # of failed projects

18% improvement in productivity

31% improvement in customer satisfaction

49% of PMOs provide project management training. [16]

Top 5 PMO Challenges:

Resistance to change within the organization

PMO is perceived as unnecessary overhead

Not enough time/resources for strategic activities

Value added by PMO is difficult to prove

Poor resource management capabilities

In Organizations Without a PMO, Projects are Managed by:

IT managers or business execs – 38%

Non-management IT staff – 26%

Project managers within IT department – 22%

Project managers outside IT department – 9%

Outsourced project managers – 1%

8. Project Failure

Only 64% of projects meet their goals.

70% of companies report having at least one failed project in the last year.

Organizations lose $109 million for every $1 billion invested in projects and programs.

High-performing organizations successfully complete 89% of projects, while low performers only complete 36%

successfully. Low performers waste nearly 12 times more resources than high-performing organizations.

Only one-third of companies always prepare a business case for new projects.

60% of companies don't measure ROI on projects.

Average Project Success Rates: 39% of all projects succeed (delivered on time, on budget, and with required features and functions)

43% are challenged (late, over budget, and/or with fewer than the required features and functions) 18% fail (either cancelled prior to completion or delivered and never used).

Average % of features delivered – 69% Average cost overrun – 59%

Average time overrun – 74%

Small Projects (less than $1 million) VS. *Large Projects* (more than $10 million)

Small Projects (less than $1 million)

76% are successful

20% are challenged

4% fail

VS.

Large Projects (more than $10 million)

10% are successful

52% are challenged

38% fail

Large projects are twice as likely to be late, over budget, and missing critical features than small projects. A large project is more than 10 times more likely to fail outright, meaning it will be cancelled or will not be used because it outlived its usefulness prior to implementation.

Most Common Causes of Project Failure: Changing priorities within organization – 40%

Inaccurate requirements – 38%

Change in project objectives – 35%

Undefined risks/opportunities – 30%

Poor communication – 30%

Undefined project goals – 30%

Inadequate sponsor support – 29%

Inadequate cost estimates – 29%

Inaccurate task time estimate – 27%

Resource dependency – 25%

Poor change management – 25%

Inadequate resource forecasting – 23%

Inexperienced project manager – 20%

Limited resources – 20%

Procrastination within team – 13%

Task dependency – 11%

Other – 9%

Despite being the top driver of project success, fewer than 2 in 3 projects had actively engaged project sponsors.

68% of projects don't have an effective project sponsor to provide clear direction or help address problems.

Projects Completed in the Last Year:

64% successfully met original goals/business objectives

62% were supported by active project sponsors

55% finished within budget

50% finished on time

44% experienced scope creep

15% were considered failures

Strategic Initiatives: Organizations report that an average of 3 out of 5 projects are not aligned with business strategy.

Only 56% of strategic initiatives meet their original goals and business intent.

44% of strategic initiatives were reported as unsuccessful. Top causes:

- Lack of executive support

- Lack of focus on key initiatives & projects that are strategically relevant

- Lack of skills and/or personnel for effective strategy implementation

Over 25% of companies don't conduct a strategic review to identify how a proposed project will benefit the business.

60% of companies don't consistently align projects with business strategy.

9 Lessons Learned from the Apollo 11 Moon Landing

"We can lick gravity, but sometimes paperwork is overwhelming." —Wernher von Braun, Chief Architect of Apollo's Saturn V

Neil Armstrong, Buzz Aldrin, and Michael Collins may have been the most visible figures of the 1969 moon landing, but the Apollo 11 team included thousands of people led by a select group of program and project managers at NASA. Tasked with the nearly impossible goal of putting an American on the moon in less than a decade, the Apollo program will always be remembered as a remarkable feat of technological innovation. And yet to many leaders at NASA, its true legacy lies in its project management achievements.

Use these 10 lessons learned from their extraordinary experiences to make your own project a stellar success.

1. Keep Open Lines of Communication with Stakeholders

"When John Kennedy went before Congress on May 25, 1961 and said we were going to the Moon, our total flight experience was one 15-minute suborbital flight." —Dr.

John M. Logsdon, Director of the Center for International Science and Technology Policy

To say Kennedy set an ambitious timeline is an understatement. The fact is, sometimes stakeholders will have sky-high expectations that you don't think are realistic. So take a cue from Dr. Robert Gilruth, Director of the Manned Spacecraft Center at the time. He recognized that he and Kennedy were working on the same team, not fighting against each other. Instead of starting his relationship with Kennedy on a tense, adversarial note, Gilruth chose honest communication. He said, "I don't know if this is possible," and followed it with frank and upfront details about the resources NASA would need in order to make the dream a reality. Gilruth recalls, "[Kennedy] really wanted us to be successful." So no matter how difficult it may be to manage your stakeholders' expectations, remind each other that you share the same goal and use that motivation to focus on the project's success.

2. Planning is the Most Important Step...

"We knew what had to be done. How to do it in 10 years was never addressed before the announcement was made. But quite simply, we considered the program a number of phases." —Dr. Maxime A. Faget, Chief Engineer & Designer of the Apollo command and lunar modules

When faced with an extraordinarily complex project, Apollo's program leaders broke it down into much smaller steps and focused on attaining each one. They set a series of milestones: phase 1 was to fly to the moon, phase 2 was to orbit the moon, phase 3 was to land an unmanned craft on the moon, and so on. They organized all their work and measured their progress around these set milestones. Had they immediately set their sights on a full-fledged lunar landing, history may have turned out very different.

In spite of the time crunch, the NASA team put a great deal of thought into the planning process, viewing it as an opportunity to cut as much risk as possible. Dr. Faget recalls, "I basically said the best way to deal with risk management is in the basic conceptual design, get the damn risk out of it." If you're facing a tight deadline you may be tempted to jump right in and get to work, but check that reflex. Take a beat and formulate a thorough project plan, considering risk from the very beginning. You'll thank yourself later!

3. ...But Don't Be Afraid to Modify the Plan

"They probably normally expected us to land with about two minutes of fuel left. And here we were, still a hundred feet above the surface, at 60 seconds." —Buzz Aldrin, Lunar Module Pilot

On descent to their landing site, the lunar module's computer became overloaded with tasks and incoming data, threatening to reboot in the middle of the landing sequence. Armstrong and Aldrin discovered they were going to miss their target, and would likely smack into a crater littered with treacherous boulders at an alarming velocity. Armstrong took semi-automatic control of the lunar module, while Aldrin fed him altitude and velocity data. They successfully landed on the moon's surface with just 25 seconds worth of fuel left. If Armstrong and Aldrin hadn't acted, Mission Control would probably have been forced to abort the mission, and Armstrong's iconic moonwalk would never have happened.

So remember that even the most well-thought-out project plans may need to be altered if circumstances change or a new opportunity arises. Don't be so rigid that you fail to adapt to either save your project from disaster or seize the chance to deliver beyond expectations.

4. Acknowledge Risk, but Don't Let It Deter You

"We said to ourselves that we have now done everything we know how to do. We feel comfortable with all of the unknowns that we went into this program with. We don't know what else to do to make this thing risk-free, so it's time to go." —Dr. Christopher C. Kraft, Jr., Director of Flight Operations

The Apollo 11 mission was perhaps one of the most risky undertakings in human history. From technical failure to human error, any number of things could have gone wrong — and did. But without acknowledging and planning for that risk, the achievement would never have been made.

NASA handled risk by actively looking for it and constantly asking themselves, "What if?" Having backup systems and procedures in place ensured there was always a Plan B. So be proactive in assessing and managing risk for your own projects. Identify situations that could trip your team up and plan for them — but don't let an acceptable amount of risk keep you from pushing ahead.

Another risk management strategy embraced by NASA: training and empowering your team to make good decisions and fix problems on the fly. Howard Tindall says, "I think one of the greatest contributors to minimizing risk was the extraordinary amount of training that was done. That really saved us many, many times because I don't think there was a single mission that we didn't have some significant failures. The fact was that people could figure them out because they had been trained and knew how to work with each other."

5. Be Strategic About Team Communication

"One of the biggest challenges that we had was one of communication and coordination." —Owen Morris, Chief Engineer & Manager of the Lunar Module

Apollo's team of project managers went from managing small projects with a select team of close colleagues to managing thousands of people they had never met. Coordinating such a massive effort required constant communication to avoid costly or dangerous errors. Their solution was to identify five central priorities and drill them into every single level of the organization. With the entire team aligned around those set priorities, communication and discipline became infinitely easier. Team leaders also met every few weeks to coordinate efforts, discuss progress, explain current challenges, and work together to overcome problems. At no point was any team in the dark about what another group was doing, or what support they needed.

Communication is often cited as the #1 reason projects fail, so take a proactive approach. Don't just trust that communication among team members will fall into place on its own, or that everyone will assume the same priorities. Create a plan for how your team will communicate with each other and with you, and check in frequently to offer support, clarify high-priority tasks, and make sure processes are running smoothly.

6. Delegate!

"Another thing that was extraordinary was how things were delegated down. NASA responsibilities were delegated to people who didn't know how to do these things, and were expected to go find out how to do it." — Howard W. TIndall, Jr., Mission Technique Coordinator

Delegating to people who don't have experience with a certain task may seem counterintuitive, but it was something Apollo project managers actively encouraged — in fact, the average age of the entire Operations team was just 26, most fresh out of college. NASA gave someone a problem and the freedom to run with it, and the results speak for themselves.

So while it's tempting to give important tasks only to team members who have direct experience, you may be missing out if you do. While you shouldn't just dump a critical task on a hapless employee and wish them good luck, with the proper support, fresh eyes and curious minds can discover the most innovative solutions to a problem — or find valuable ways to improve stale processes.

7. Record Lessons Learned

"When we had the [Apollo 1] fire, we took a step back and said okay, what lessons have we learned from this horrible tragedy? Now let's be doubly sure that we are going to do it right the next time. And I think that fact right there is what allowed us to get Apollo done in the '60s." —Dr. Christopher C. Kraft, Jr., Director of Flight Operations

The Apollo program was home to some of the most brilliant minds in the world, and yet no one was shy about their mistakes. They made recording and learning from their errors a central part of their process, from the very top of the organization down. Failure was simply an opportunity to learn and improve.

Follow their lead by making retrospectives an ongoing part of your project, not a one-time event that's relegated to the end. Collect lessons learned at each standup or status meeting to refine your process as you go, and take the lead yourself so your team knows it's safe to discuss mistakes and roadblocks without judgment. Your team — and your project's results — will be that much stronger for it.

8. Celebrate Success as a Team

"We would like to give special thanks to all those Americans who built the spacecraft; who did the construction, design, the tests, and put their hearts and all their abilities into those craft. To those people tonight, we give a special thank you." —Neil Armstrong, July 26 television broadcast from orbit

At every opportunity the astronauts called the world's attention to the efforts of their teammates back on the ground. So when you deliver a successful project to a group of happy stakeholders, share that applause with the rest of your team. Relay positive feedback and results back to the group, acknowledge their hard work with a round of high-fives, and use small wins throughout the project to fuel continued hard work.

9. Make Project Success Sustainable

"The leader has got to really believe in his organization, and believe that they can do things, and find ways to challenge them." —Dr. Maxime A. Faget, Chief Engineer & designer of the Apollo command and lunar modules

Once you've achieved success, how do you make it repeatable across your entire organization? According to Apollo's project managers, every successful project needs three things: the first is a vivid picture of where you're going and what you can accomplish to motivate your team. Second: complete commitment from leadership so your team has the support they need to get things done. And finally, a deadline or goal to keep everyone focused on high-priority tasks that further immediate business goals. Secure these three things at the beginning of a new project and you're already on the path to success.

Keys to Project Management Success

As experienced project managers, we know you have some expert tips on managing projects and achieving results that are out of this world. Share your best advice with fellow readers in the comments below!

7 Top Challenges by Peter Taylor

Project manager, author, and speaker Peter Taylor is famous for the "work smarter, not harder" philosophy he advocates in *The Lazy Project Manager*. In his new book, *Real Project Management*, Taylor surveys both new and experienced project managers to identify their top challenges and offer his characteristic brand of efficient and effective solutions. Between his astute observations of the past, present, and future of project management, and his genius tips for combating common management challenges, Taylor's new book gets our enthusiastic recommendation. Watch our recent interview with Peter Taylor for a quick introduction to the author and his area of project management expertise.

We've collected seven of Taylor's tips for project managers to give you a peek at what lies between the pages of *Real Project Management*:

Challenge 1: Poor Communication

Good communication has always been a sticking point for project managers, but it's getting even trickier to get right. Thanks to always-on technology and social media, an endless stream of messages are coming in from a multitude of channels. Which communication tools should you use, when, and for what purpose?

Taylor's Tip: Good communication means the right message, at the right time, in the right format. Consider all three aspects when you have something important to say. But before you hit send, also consider whether your message really needs to be communicated at all. Eliminating unnecessary or distracting communication will help make sure important messages are received loud and clear.

Challenge 2: Virtual Nature of Projects

With remote teams on the rise, it's important for project managers to understand that who you're communicating to is just as important as the message itself. We must always remember to take cultural differences into account, but great project managers also factor in the loss of other communication cues like tone of voice and body language. They consider how their messages could be read, not just how they *intend* them to be read. The use of emoticons and other informal language is becoming a common way to eliminate misunderstandings and foster good working relationships.

Taylor's Tip: Cultural differences go far beyond language barriers; they affect how people approach their work and what they value. That's why good people skills are needed now more than ever — not only to manage distributed teams, but also to effectively argue why you need certain resources, why particular tasks should be prioritized, demonstrate business justification, and so on. So don't neglect your soft skills!

Challenge 3: Constant Time Pressures

For project managers, the clock is always ticking. Time to deadline, time to market, time to achieving a certain ROI — all are expected to be fast, fast, and faster. Taylor sees expectation management as the key to success, since mismatched expectations mean wasted time. You need to thoroughly understand what it is you're expected to deliver in order to plan the most efficient path to delivering it.

Taylor's Tip: There's a difference between working hard and being effective. Don't create extra work for yourself by needlessly involving yourself in decisions, communications, or processes that don't really need your input. It's not only a poor use of your time and energy, it slows down your team!

Challenge 4: Executive Support

Taylor sees a lack of committed project sponsors as a major challenge facing today's project managers. But a big part of the problem is this: while 99.5% of organizations surveyed said they believe good project sponsorship is essential to project success, 83% admitted they do nothing to develop, train, or support project sponsors within their companies.

Taylor's Tip: Until organizations start properly supporting project sponsors, project managers will need to take it upon themselves to communicate their needs to their sponsors. Make sure your project sponsor understands how crucial they are to the project's success, what their role is, and what's expected of them.

Challenge 5: Strategic Connection

It's not enough to successfully manage your projects; you need to understand the overall business strategy connecting them all (what Taylor calls "strategic connection"). One-off or "orphan" projects only drain company resources, so overall business strategy should be something that's well understood throughout the company, not just at the executive level. Every project manager (and their team members) should be free to question whether or how the project they're working on contributes to larger business objectives. And if the connection can't be proven, the project should be halted.

Taylor's Tip: Project managers must move beyond the tactical approach of managing budgets, project scope, and everyday processes to a more strategic view, where they focus on how their project can deliver the most business value.

Challenge 6: Increased Complexity

Projects are becoming more and more complex. Taylor defines a complex project as one that has some degree of uncertainty either surrounding its process or its purpose: perhaps there are unclear goals, various political factors or influences, or the tools and processes being used are new to the team. Whatever the root cause, complexity often means increased risk, and unprepared project managers may be in for a struggle.

Taylor's Tip: Junior and mid-level project managers should seek out opportunities to work on more complex projects under senior project managers, learning all they can from the experience so they can confidently manage complexity in future work.

Challenge 7: Lessons Learned

Although each project manager and team member has personal takeaways from each project, they're too likely to internalize them and not share them with their colleagues. Even teams that actually have an internal knowledge base are often unsure what is (or isn't) helpful advice, a valuable template, a best practice, and so on. Plus, there's always pressure to start work on the next project as soon as the first is finished, skipping or rushing the process of reflecting, recording, and sharing potentially valuable information.

Taylor's Tip: Instead of trying to record all lessons learned from a project, ask your colleagues what information they would find most helpful. Do they want to know what risks others encountered & overcame? Start a knowledge base just for people to record the risks they experienced and their advice. Whether it's useful templates, effective processes, or project planning tips, find out what your team wants and focus on that.

More Tips for Today's Project Managers

Check out our interview with Peter Taylor to learn the new definition of project success, which types of projects are most costly for organizations, and much more — straight from the man himself.

5 Lessons to Learn from Superheroes

With busy schedules, tight deadlines and many other day-to-day project management challenges, have you ever wished you had a super power to help you cope with them all in a magical way? Inspired by interesting comments to our CEO's recent post "7 Business Lessons an Entrepreneur Can Learn from Superheroes", we thought of a few lessons a project manager can learn from superheroes.

1. Thor – Learn humility

This Northern god of Thunder was thrown down to Earth and deprived of his powers, until he *proved to be humble*. Jim Collins, the author of leadership best-sellers *Good to Great* and *Built to Last*, also suggests humility as a key factor of being a great team leader. As an example, he writes about Darwin Smith, CEO of Kimberly-Clark. Described as a "shy, unpretentious, even awkward" guy, he turned Kimberly-Clark into the leading consumer paper products company in the world during his 20 years as a CEO.

2. Spider-Man – Take responsibility

Peter Parker learned the hard way that *"With great power comes great responsibility."* Of course, a project manager doesn't need to save New York from scientists who go crazy, but a project's success is definitely a big weight that lies on their shoulders.However, as Ian McAllister, senior traffic manager at Amazon, mentions in his answer to this Quora question, taking responsibility is different from taking blame. Just remember, that at the end of the day, it doesn't matter whose fault it was, but that it's your responsibility to prevent the mistake from happening in the future.By the way, responsibility has an upside as well. Our recent survey showed that more than 80% of managers consider a **sense of responsibility the no.1 productivity motivator** for them!

3. Green Lantern – Be creative

A project manager can learn a thing or two from Hal Jordan who used his ring to materialize things that existed in his mind. When competition is hot, you need to be extra creative to get ahead of it. Edward de Bono, the author of the "lateral thinking" term (which is a less-used substitute to the "outside-the-box" buzzword) said, "Creative thinking is not a talent; it is a skill that can be learnt. It empowers people by adding strength to their natural abilities which improves teamwork, productivity and where appropriate profits."

4. The Thing – Stay empathic

Don't let appearance mislead you, this thick-skinned guy may seem tough, but he is the heart and soul of Fantastic Four. He possesses the trait that Dr. Daniel Goleman, famous psychologist and science journalist, finds **mission-critical for a successful leader** – *empathy*. "Leaders with empathy," says Goleman, "do more than sympathize with people around them: they use their knowledge to improve their companies in subtle, but important ways." This doesn't mean that they agree with everyone's view or try to please everybody. Rather, they "thoughtfully consider employees' feelings – along with other factors – in the process of making intelligent decisions."

5. Professor X – Raise superheroes yourself

Probably the best team manager in the Marvel universe, Professor Charles Xavier, didn't only build a famous X-team, but also created a school where he helped gifted youngsters safely develop their powers. As a team leader, it's one of your priorities to **foster and improve your team member's talents** and skills. After all, this is the way to building a dream superhero team.